BEING HUMAN
BEING HOPEFUL

Walter L. Underwood

ABINGDON PRESS
NASHVILLE

BEING HUMAN, BEING HOPEFUL

Copyright © 1987 by Abingdon Press

This book is printed on acid-free paper.

Library of Congress Cataloging-in-Publication Data

Underwood, Walter L. (Walter Lee), 1925–
  Being human, being hopeful.
  1. Consolation. I. Title.
BV4905.2.U64   1987   248.8'6   86-25849

ISBN 0-687-02815-9 (alk. paper)

Scripture quotations noted RSV are from the Revised Standard Version of
the Bible, copyrighted 1946, 1952, © 1971, 1973 by the Division of
Christian Education of the National Council of the Churches of Christ in
the U.S.A. and are used by permission.
  Those noted Phillips are from The New Testament in Modern English,
copyright © J.B. Phillips 1958, 1959, 1960, 1972.
  All others are from the King James Version of the Bible.

Lines from "Heresy Indeed" (p. 81) are used by permission of the author,
Sara Henderson Hay.

MANUFACTURED BY THE PARTHENON PRESS AT
NASHVILLE, TENNESSEE, UNITED STATES OF AMERICA

This one is for
Don, Ron, and Wally,
Bobby and Mary Lou

C O N T E N T S

Despite the vast diversity of age, race, nationality, background, environment, education, and experience, all people share one attribute equally—our humanity. The commonality of our humanness should provide all of us with a distinct empathetic understanding of one another. Whatever else divides us, our humanness unites us. Whatever else alienates us, our shared humanity bonds us together.

The themes of these discourses are relevant to all human beings, simply because we are human. All of us are subject to this human predicament, to a lesser or greater degree, at some point in our lives. There are few of us who can honestly attest to avoiding any of these themes, much less all of them. Sooner or later we all shall be victims of worry, fear, stress, loneliness, depression, failure, rejection, doubt, despair, guilt, discontent, death.

This book is one person's attempt to discover God's solutions to our human predicament.

MATTHEW 6:31

Worry. "Don't worry!" is one of the most startling commands in the New Testament. In effect, Jesus says to us, "Don't be anxious about anything. God takes care of the birds of the air. He takes care of the lilies of the field. Why don't you believe he'll take care of you? Do not worry!"

That's not only a tall order, but to many of us it also may seem rationally impossible and totally impractical. Is Jesus really asking us not to worry, when people on every street corner are crying for help? The number of young people who commit suicide has increased alarmingly; drugs and alcohol can be found in almost every high school, yet Jesus tells us not to be anxious. Our crime rate is increasing: Murder, rape, theft, acts of all kinds of violence are escalating, and we are told not to worry. When one person out of every ten shows signs of severe mental illness, millions of people go to bed hungry every night, and terrorism runs rampant, how can we not be burdened with anxiety? Does Jesus really mean we are not to worry in the face of instantaneous mass destruction? If he does, we might say, "Well, after all, Jesus, we're only human. We're not divine like you, nor are we superpeople. These concerns, in addition to our personal problems, are very real. How can you possibly tell us not to worry?"

Someone once said that the best way to stop worrying is to turn off your radio and television and stop reading the newspapers. A cartoonist accurately sketched the tenor of current events when he depicted a television announcer saying, "The following program contains news of the day—viewer discretion advised." Indeed, the news commentaries of today are guaranteed to give us many a sleepless night.

Let me qualify Jesus' command by saying that, in all probability, it was not meant for inveterate worriers. Most of us know people who thoroughly enjoy worrying. These men and women carry their worries around with them as they do their wallets or purses. They wouldn't give up their worries if they could. Many of them really do not want to be free of anxiety because their worries are the most fun they have in life. They are like the gloomy man at the party.

Someone noticed his dejection and asked, "Why are you so worried? Everyone else is having a good time."

"I'm worried," the man replied, "because there might be a party somewhere else where they're having more fun." Some people simply relish worry.

However, let's put the chronic worriers aside and think about the people who are usually normal, healthy, and happy. To them, Jesus is saying, "You're not supposed to worry." That's still a difficult command in a world like ours.

There is one other point we should be aware of before attempting to deal with the problem of worry. Not all worry is bad—some of it is both good and necessary. Carl Michalson once said that nothing significant is ever accomplished without worry, because worry spurs us to action and promotes conditions favorable to the carrying out of our commitments, thus reaffirming the fact that we are supposed to worry about some things. For instance, you'd better be worried enough to seek medical assistance if you have a severe pain in your abdomen. If you have a sharp pain in the region of your heart, you need to call a doctor. There are definitely some things we should worry about. Quite obviously, certain areas of our personal and professional lives should receive our attention and concern.

When a young boy went into a drugstore one day to use the telephone, the pharmacist overheard his conversation.

The boy dialed a number and asked, "Sir, have you filled that job yet? . . . Oh, you have. Well, is the boy doing a good job?" He paused a moment to listen to the response, then thanked the person at the other end of the line and hung up.

The pharmacist said, "I'm sorry you didn't get the job."

"Oh," the boy replied, "I got the job two days ago. I was just worried about how I was doing." That kind of worry is good.

But excessive worry is destructive, both physically and spiritually. Many of us have stomach ulcers due, in large part, to too much worry. Others suffer extreme physical distress primarily caused by worry. Our body's response to debilitating worry can range from irritating skin rashes to disabling illnesses. And anxiety also destroys our mental and emotional health. We have nervous breakdowns, require countless hours of counseling, gulp millions of tranquilizers, and endure extended hospitalization because of worry. In addition, immoderate worry destroys the spiritual vitality of our lives. It has been said that worry is not merely weakness, but wickedness. That is true, because worry is actually an atheistic stance. If we worry excessively, it indicates that we believe God has abdicated and it's up to us to hold our lives and the world together.

Now let us attempt to deal with this problem. If, like many of us, you have a tendency to worry too much, it is helpful to remember that most of the things we fret about never happen. James Russell Lowell said, "Remember that the misfortunes hardest to bear are those which never come" (*Democracy and Addresses by James Russell Lowell,* 1884). We worry in anticipation of so very many things that never occur. Repeatedly, I have found myself counseling with those who worry in anticipation of something that might happen but often never does.

One man overcame this problem in a very practical way by developing what he called a "worry table." He wrote down all the things he was worried about, then classified them. He quickly discovered that 40 percent of the time, he was worrying about the possibility of disasters; during 30 percent, he stewed about decisions he had already made; 12 percent was devoted to fretting about becoming ill or having a nervous breakdown; 10 percent, he was troubled about his friends and their children; and 8 percent of the time he worried about immediate problems he needed to solve. After reviewing his worry table, it became obvious that he could discard 92 percent of all his worries. Aren't we like that? We worry in anticipation of things that may never happen. If each of us took time to make a similar list, we probably would discover that only about 8 percent of our worries are valid.

British industrialist and film maker J. Arthur Rank lived a complex, hurried life, yet he too found a workable solution to his worry problem. He formed a worry club; he was the sole member of what he called the Wednesday Worry Club. Whenever he had a concern, he wrote it down and put it in a box. Every Wednesday afternoon, he took the worries out of the box and read them. By that time, most were no longer apropos and he would throw them away. He had only a few worries left. When someone asked what he did with those remaining worries, Sir Arthur replied that he put them back in the box so the Wednesday Worry Club could handle them the next Wednesday. That took care of his excessive worry.

There is a fascinating story about a village paralyzed by the fear that a monster on top of a nearby mountain was about to destroy it. The monster was gigantic. It had the head of a crocodile, the body of a hippopotamus, and the tail of an enormous snake. It breathed fiery smoke. The villagers, certain that the monster was going to destroy them, completely stopped working and playing; essentially, they gave up living. They spent their time moaning and wailing, waiting for the dreadful destruction to come.

A little boy in the village decided that if he were going to die anyway, he might as well find out for himself what the monster looked like. So he slipped away from his parents and began to climb the mountain. As he ascended its rocky cliffs, the monster seemed to grow smaller and smaller. When he was halfway up, the monster looked a great deal smaller than it had at the foot of the mountain.

The boy thought to himself, "Why is it that the closer I get, the smaller the monster becomes?" Finally, when he reached the mountain's peak, he discovered the monster—a quiet little creature about the size of a frog. The boy took the creature home with him and kept it as a pet.

Isn't that tale a metaphor for many of our own worries? While we uneasily anticipate them, they seem to be huge monsters. But the more closely we examine them, the more insignificant they become until quite often they amount to nothing at all.

I would like to recommend another method for dealing with excessive worry: We should try to replace our worries with our blessings. A simple exercise for accomplishing this is called imaging. As an example, suppose you are worried about being too tired to go to work in the morning. If you image that in your subconscious, it can consume your thinking and your heart. Rather than thinking, "I won't be able to go to the office in the morning!" replace that picture with a pleasurable image. What is one of your favorite pastimes? Do you like to snorkel, shop for antiques, read a current novel? If skiing is your pet avocation, imagine that you will fly to Aspen this week. You'll spend tomorrow morning swishing down the slopes, then you'll enjoy the evening in front of a warm fire.

Think what a pleasurable image that is. And as long as you can image that wonderful ski trip in your mind, there's no room to image the worry that you may not be able to go to work. You cannot image both, and you do have control over the image you place in your mind.

When we worry, we keep a picture in our minds of negative thoughts, both past and present. The more we image a worry, the more we create tension; the more tension we have, the more we create worry. Thus we are caught in a vicious, unrelenting cycle which we cannot seem to break. But you can choose to image in your mind the blessings of your life: friends, family, being alive, health, a good job, opportunities for the future. You can break the worry habit by substituting the blessings for the worry. The next time you start to worry, think of a red flag to remind you that you have an opportunity to change the image in your mind. Then rehearse your blessings instead of your worries. "As a man thinketh in his heart, so is he." The image you retain in your mind and heart makes a vast difference.

Finally, we should try to replace fear with faith. When we worry, we're really fearing something that will happen. We're afraid something terrible is going to occur. Worry really is fear, is it not?

A medical doctor once remarked to E. Stanley Jones that people who worry excessively die sooner than people who don't. He added that he did not know why.

"I think I know," Jones replied. "I am inwardly fashioned for faith and not for fear. Fear is not my native land; faith is. . . . In anxiety and worry my being is gasping for breath. . . . But in faith and confidence I breathe freely. . . . To live by worry is to live against Reality" (*Abundant Living* [1942], p. 85). How true! We're made for faith, not fear, and we should replace our fear with faith. The atmosphere of faith is the one in which we breathe more easily.

Excessive worry is such a pathetic revelation of our lack of faith. It means we do not believe we have a heavenly Father, a God to trust, to cast our cares upon. Yet, the Bible is clear: "Cast all your anxieties on him, for he cares about you. . . . Thou dost keep him in perfect peace, whose mind is stayed on thee, because he trusts in thee" (I Pet. 5:7; Isa. 26:3 RSV).

In the end, being able to rid ourselves of worry comes down to a matter of faith, of trust. When we have done our best, when there is nothing more we can do, then we should cast our worries on God. Let God carry them. He provides for the birds in the air and the lilies in the field; will he not also care for our needs?

The tycoon J. C. Penney suffered tremendous financial losses during the depression. He worried about this to such an extent that he had a nervous breakdown and was confined to a sanitarium for months. The doctors worked with him to no avail. He became increasingly worse until one night he decided he was near death, and he wrote farewell notes to each of his loved ones.

The next morning, to his great surprise, he was still breathing. And although he could scarcely believe it, he heard the sound of music. Struggling out of bed, he walked down the corridor, where he found a group of people having a prayer meeting. They were singing:

Be not dismayed what e'er betide,
God will take care of you;
Beneath his wings of love abide,
God will take care of you.

Mr. Penney remembered that old song from his childhood. It evoked within him an overwhelming sense of the care, the kindness, the love of Almighty God. He suddenly began to image his blessings instead of his worries. He planted in his subconscious mind and heart the blessings of his loved ones; the blessings of his family, friends, and business associates who had stood by him; the blessings of opportunities that still lay ahead. That enabled him to replace his fear with faith. He realized that God did care, that he could cast his cares upon God, that God would take care of him. A belief once dead was alive again. From that moment, his healing became so rapid his doctors marveled at his recovery. Soon he was well and returned to his work. He lived to be ninety-five, but he never forgot the old song that enabled him to image his blessings instead of his worries, to replace his fear with his faith.

The J. B. Phillips version translates Philippians 4:6-7 like this: "Don't worry over anything whatever; . . . tell God every detail of your needs in thankful prayer, and the peace of God, which surpasses human understanding, will keep constant guard over your hearts and minds as they rest in Christ Jesus."

The assurance of that promise enables us to replace our worries with our blessings and live a life essentially free of worry, just as Jesus instructed us.

LUKE 10:38-42

Stress.

Most of us are familiar with the frequently quoted comment, "Most men lead lives of quiet desperation." That was Henry David Thoreau's judgment of life in the early part of the nineteenth century. If Thoreau were living today, he would doubtless revise his observation: "Most men, women, and oftentimes children, lead lives of quiet desperation."

Our desperation, the stress we feel, is caused not only by our work—the pressure to excel, to succeed, to compete—but also by family problems and our inability to manage our personal relationships. Our defeats, our failures, and our disappointments cause stress. Stress also results from sorrow—over a death, illness, divorce, retirement, or a dozen other occurrences. It is even experienced by some—especially the young—who think we are perhaps in the last days of civilization, facing the end of the world.

Whatever the cause, stress begins with frustration, which leads to loneliness, which leads to depression, which leads to franticness, which leads to desperation, which finally eventuates in total despair. Every age has a name, and some are calling ours the Age of Stress. Americans now consume more than twenty thousand tons of aspirin a year. That's two-thirds of an aspirin every day for each American, which means that most of us must have a headache nearly all the time. That does not include the tranquilizers and other medications we gobble in large doses.

It's even difficult to joke about this problem. It has been said that humor is a revelation of what we're really concerned about. You will notice that when we joke about stress, there is a tragic undertone of realistic truth that almost seeks to destroy our attempted levity. A "Peanuts" cartoon shows Peppermint Patty and Marcie in bed. The window is open; it's a very dark night.

Peppermint Patty is saying, "I can't sleep for thinking about what the speaker said. I'm scared. What if the world ends tonight, Marcie?"

Marcie replies, "I promise there'll be a tomorrow, sir. In fact, it's already tomorrow in Australia."

"But," Peppermint Patty protests, "he said we're in the last days."

"Go to sleep, sir," Marcie suggests. "The sun is shining in Australia." Even in our humor there is a worrisome, tragic truth that indicates our stress is real.

Life is very often like a merry-go-round, and with each succeeding turn, it goes faster and faster until it becomes difficult to hold on. Someone is thrown off with each turn. Viewing that, we become desperate, lest on the next turn, it is we who will be thrown off.

In Luke 10:38-42, Jesus is on the way to Jerusalem to be crucified. He stops by the house of Mary and

Martha, two people who love him and whom he loves. He only wants to sit in an easy chair, prop his feet up, and try to relax; to meditate, pray, and ready himself for the ordeal ahead. But as soon as he enters the house, Martha prepares to entertain him. She thinks he needs a hearty dinner, so she scurries off to the kitchen to get out the china, silver, and goblets, and fix a six-course meal. Mary is just sitting in the living room with Jesus, being quiet and supportive. This makes Martha very angry.

Finally she bursts through the kitchen door, saying, "Lord, don't you see me in there working, trying to get this dinner together? Why don't you make Mary come in and help me instead of just sitting?"

Jesus replies, "You missed the point altogether, Martha. It's not a full course meal I need. It's the solitude, the quiet, the support of your love. You're too stressful about something that really doesn't matter." That advice also applies to us. Don't we often find ourselves being too stressful about something that actually is insignificant?

However, some degree of urgency, some stress, is essential. I'm glad Martha thought about feeding Jesus, or he might have gone hungry. It was beneficial that she had enough stress to remember he needed to eat, and in like manner, some stress is both essential and beneficial for all of us.

A fine concert piano has 243 strings, so taut they effect a 40,000-pound pull on the piano's frame. Without that stress the piano would not play in tune. As human beings, we too need some stress. For instance, a sprinter poised at the starting block should have some stress or he will not win the race. A doctor at Yale University has said that the worst surgery patients are either those who feel no stress before surgery or those who feel too much. The best prospect for successful surgery is a person who has a normal, realistic sense of anxiety, fear, and stress about the impending operation.

Yet each of us must discover the appropriate amount of pressure, because too much stress is dangerous—physically, emotionally, and spiritually. According to recent statistics, 25 percent of all Americans have some form of hypertension. Two persons die every minute from hypertension or related causes. Men living today die of heart attacks thirteen years sooner than their fathers did. Stress provokes all kinds of physical ailments: insomnia, headache, backache, fatigue, nervous exhaustion, difficulty in breathing, lack of energy, digestive upsets, and other problems. Stress can even make you grind your teeth in your sleep. The Methodist Hospital in Houston has a sleep laboratory, where the sole purpose is to examine and try to find cures, in large part, for people who are under stress during their sleep.

Just as an overloaded electrical circuit in a house can finally blow out all the lights, our human fuse blows out when overloaded with too much pressure. Psychologically, undue stress creates a huge ripple in our psyches, often the precursor of serious mental illness. And it threatens us spiritually because stress is destructive to our spiritual wholeness, peace of mind, inner contentment, and happiness. Undue stress can even cause us to lose our faith in God. Many times I have counseled with persons under such great stress that they say they no longer believe in the goodness of God.

But despite its evident pervasiveness and the dreadful toll it can take, there are several ways we can learn to manage stress. First of all, we need to rid life of its emotional poisons, because stress is often the result of destructive venoms that become lodged in the interior of our hearts, minds, and souls.

One afternoon when I was seventeen, I was struck with a severe pain in my abdomen. I suffered for several hours. Finally I called a friend. He summoned a professor who brought me some hot tea. The pain was so excruciating that at last they called a doctor. The doctor poked me once in the stomach.

He said, "You have a bad appendix. It has to come out immediately. I'm calling the hospital to arrange surgery."

Had my appendix ruptured before it was removed, it would have discharged poisons into my body that might have killed me. Those physical poisons are deadly, but the interior emotional poisons we often collect—hatred, envy, jealousy, greed, bitterness, resentment—often combine to build high levels of stress that are destructive.

There is no point in dealing with the external problems of our stress until we have dealt with the interior problems. We are tempted to think that external problems are causing our stress. We think, "It's my job . . . my boss . . . my co-workers. It must be the other people I have to work with, or the annoying neighbor down the block." We blame somebody or something else in order to avoid dealing with the real problem. When we do that, we lie to ourselves. Before we blame external problems for our stress, we should start on the inside. We should look honestly at the interior of our lives and find the poisons there—hatred, envy, jealousy, greed, bitterness, resentment. We must get rid of those poisons.

Another stress neutralizer is a life filled with fun. I've chosen the word *fun* deliberately. I refer to the kind of fun that is re-creative and regenerative.

The natural world seems to understand this theory. Trees, grass, flowers, soil—even the water table of the earth—understand that they are the beneficiaries of certain re-creative, regenerative powers and strengths which flow to them because of the very nature of their existence and the nature of the universe. But as humans, we often make the mistake of thinking we do not need external regeneration, that we can spend and expend ourselves without replenishing our strength, give out and never take in. That is like driving a car but never stopping to refuel. Finally, the car just won't run. And a human being just won't continue to run unless he or she takes the time to refuel, to take in, to replace what has been expended.

Physical exercise is one method of re-creating and regenerating ourselves. Once we become accustomed to a regular program of physical exercise, many of us discover we actually need it.

Hobbies and avocations also are invaluable aids in relieving tension. Reading something other than professionally related material is beneficial. Detective stories don't happen to be my favorite form of reading material, but I know people who love them and find great re-creative fun in reading who-dun-its.

Serving others is also a way to add fun to our lives—re-creative, regenerative fun—because much of our stress is the result of overconcern for ourselves. When we get out and care for someone who really has a need, our giving becomes a re-creative, regenerative agent.

In addition, we need to live one day at a time. We cannot carry the mistakes of the past, the fears of the future, and the problems of the present all at one time. A bridge is not engineered to support the total weight of all the cars and trucks that pass over it during a full week. It is engineered to support only so many cars and trucks at a time. If we pile a week's load of vehicles on top of one another, the bridge will collapse. And so it is with humans. We were made by God and engineered to live one day at a time. If we pile yesterday and tomorrow onto today, then we break down. We are supposed to carry only one day at a time. Jesus said, "Today's troubles are sufficient for today." Indeed they are. He was saying that we cannot carry yesterday and tomorrow and today, because that is an unbearable load. The stress is just too much.

I once heard a story about a philosophical clock. A marvelous grandfather clock was manufactured and sent to its first owner.

As it began to tick, it mused, "I am going to tick twice every second. Therefore I must tick 120 times a minute, 7,200 times an hour, and 172,800 times every 24 hours. That means I must tick 63,072,000 times a year. Why," said the clock, "in 10 years I will have to tick 630,720,000 times!" And with that, the clock had a nervous breakdown.

The owner took the clock to a repairman. When he was finally able to diagnose the trouble and repair the clock, it was returned to its owner. By this time, the clock had done some more philosophical thinking.

It said, "You know, even though I must tick 630,720,000 times in the next 10 years, I only have to tick one tick at a time." And after 100 years the clock is still ticking, one tick at a time.

That's what we are supposed to do. It is the only way we can handle stress.

I have a friend who is under extreme pressure. I once asked him how he managed it.

He answered, "I do not worry about yesterday or anticipate tomorrow. Each day I do the best I can. I give it all I have, and at night I turn it over to God."

You can't beat that for a truly biblical understanding of what Jesus is saying to us. "Today's troubles are sufficient for today."

Finally, we must keep in touch with God, for he is the source of inspiration, peace, and power. We make a huge mistake if we think we can manage stress when we are cut off from the source of our strength and our life.

Think of a flashlight and an ordinary electric light. A flashlight has a battery and it burns just as long as the battery is good. Eventually, the battery wears out and the light will not burn. But an electric light is connected to a power station, and it will burn as long as it is connected to its source of power. Just so, our lives, to have power, to manage stress, must be in touch with the Source of all power. We must practice the spiritual disciplines of the Christian faith: the study of the

Bible, teaching and learning; the experience of worship, meditation, and prayer.

A California psychologist, Stewart Bedford, wrote a book with the unlikely title *Stress and Tiger Juice* (Scott Publications, 1980). He says that to manage stress successfully, we must stay in touch with the source of life. He discovered this by studying the Desert Fathers of the fourth century. They believed they should pray twenty minutes at a time, relaxing completely and breathing deeply. With each breath they said a short prayer: "God have mercy. . . . God give me strength. . . . God give me peace." Dr. Bedford said he, too, found that to be a helpful way to manage stress— twenty minutes of prayer, relaxing the body, breathing deeply, and a short prayer spoken with each breath. It is a way of saying we cannot manage stress unless we keep in touch with the source of life, Almighty God, as he reveals himself in Jesus Christ.

The disciples were out on a boat one day when a storm came up. The winds were heavy; the boat was listing deeply from side to side.

Frightened, the disciples turned to Jesus. "Carest thou not that we perish?"

And Jesus replied, "Peace, be still."

The storm abated; the winds died; the waves ceased; their fear vanished.

And Jesus comes to each of us, in our lives of quiet desperation, to say, "Peace, be still; peace, be still."

There is no fear in love, but perfect love casts out fear. For fear has to do with punishment, and he who fears is not perfected in love.

—I JOHN 4:18 RSV

Fear.

One noted minister receives thousands of letters each week from his vast radio and television audience.

Not long ago he said, "I have discovered from the mail I receive that the most prevalent problem among men and women today is not sorrow, and it is not sin—it is fear."

That shouldn't be too surprising. We are only human, and fear is indigenous to our humanity. The Bible understands that, for it contains more than five hundred references to fear. Biblical writers obviously knew that fear is a prevailing problem.

Who could deny that all of us are frightened at one time or another? A mother fears for her children, a father is frightened his business will not go well. Many of us fear we will lose our jobs. All of us fear that someone we love may be snatched away from us. We fear the past; we fear the present; we fear the future. We fear poverty, disaster, and disgrace. We fear pain, illness, bereavement, and failure. We fear cancer, insanity, and growing old. We fear something; we fear everything. But often we fear only fear.

Seventy-five different phobias are listed in the dictionary, all the way from acrophobia, fear of heights, to neophobia, fear of the new, and phobophobia, the fear of fear itself. That is simply further indication that fear is one of the most common problems facing us today. Someone has accurately said that more people suffer from "scarecoma" than from glaucoma, from "fearosis" than sclerosis, and from "apprehendicitis" than appendicitis. It is true that we are fearful people.

Since fear is almost endemic to our society, we should be aware of how dangerous it can be. It can jeopardize our physical health by increasing the flow of adrenaline, raising blood pressure, and perhaps causing nausea or insomnia. Many other alarming results of fear can affect our bodily functions. One of the leading research specialists has said he believes cancer is sometimes caused by fear and stress. In addition, two researchers in New York have catalogued their rationale for believing that cancer can be caused by fear.

Another result of fear is emotional and mental collapse, a nervous breakdown. Furthermore, spiritual breakdown can occur when we lose our faith because of our fears. If you have ever been truly afraid, you have some understanding of what can happen to us physically, mentally, emotionally, and spiritually as the result of fear.

We can be helped enormously when we realize that the things we fear usually never happen. Most of us have had our imaginations run wild with fright at times. A friend was awakened one night about 2:00 A.M. by one of his children who tiptoed into his bedroom.

"Daddy, there's someone in the living room!"

My friend's response was, "Oh, go back to sleep."

About that time, one of his other children came in. "Daddy, there's somebody in the living room!"

So he got up, listened, and sure enough, he could hear someone in the living room. He didn't want to appear cowardly in front of his children, so he put on his robe and quietly crept downstairs. Fearing he was about to be shot or stabbed, he went to the living room and flipped on the light. The children had left some jumping beans in a bowl, and as they popped around, it sounded just as if someone were moving around.

That incident reminds me of one of my father's favorite stories. Once a wife shook her husband in the middle of the night.

"Zeb, wake up! I just heard somebody come in the house."

He turned to her and said, "If you'll be real quiet and lie still, in a little while you'll hear him go out."

That's my kind of bravery. You see, when we start to imagine, our fears can run wild. Shakespeare once wrote, "Or in the night, imagining some fear, How easy is a bush suppos'd a bear!" (*Midsummer-Night's Dream*, act 5. sc. 1. lines 21-22). We all have seen bushes that appeared to be bears.

However, despite our vivid imaginings, most of our fears never happen. Emerson poetically reminds us of this:

Some of your hurts you have cured,
And the sharpest you still have survived,
But what torments of grief you endured
From evils that never arrived!
                        —"Borrowing"

On the other hand, fear can be a friend, and it often is. The survival of life itself is dependent upon our cultivation of healthy fears. My wife and I taught our sons to be afraid of playing with matches. We taught them to fear busy intersections, rattlesnakes, bottles labeled POISON, and many other harmful things. Fear that alerts us to exercise precaution and use common sense can be a friend, and at times our survival actually depends upon it.

Another beneficial aspect of fear is that good things may come to pass because of it. For example, because some people feared tyranny, they came to the shores of America and established a democracy based on justice. Visiting citizens of other countries sometimes ask for asylum because they fear the consequences of going back to their native land. This has been the beginning of a whole new life for countless thousands.

And sometimes our fear can enable us to accomplish things that otherwise would have been impossible. In Fort Worth, Texas, a boy was working on his car in his front yard. While he was under the car, the jack broke and the car fell on him. When he screamed, his mother rushed from the house. That fragile 100-pound woman had been chronically ill most of her life. Normally, she couldn't have lifted a 25-pound sack of anything, but under the stimulus of fear, she lifted the corner of a 3,000-pound automobile to free her son. There are times when fear can, indeed, be a friend.

In some instances, fear also can be a spur to knowledge. Many of the advances of civilization were made possible by fear, and the increase in the quality and quantity of life often has been due to our fear. Because we fear disease, thousands of technicians and doctors are engaged in medical research. Because of our fear of hunger, we not only practice conservation but continually invent new ways to produce food so that no people in the world will go hungry.

On a more personal level, my fear of failing physics motivated me to learn a lot more about the subject than I ever wanted to know. A similar fear has probably served as a learning stimulus for many people. One of my schoolmates came from a very poor background; no members of his family could read or even write their names. His fear of being illiterate prodded him until he earned a doctorate and today is a professor in a great university. Fear can be a spur to knowledge and continued growth.

When we think of fear in relation to faith, it is interesting to note that while fear can be a stimulus to faith, it also can destroy faith. For instance, a singer who is scared to death may discover that fear can clutch the vocal chords so that not a note will emerge.

You may have observed that fear often grips people who are being married. Many years ago, a groom fainted during a ceremony I was performing. Now I always carry a bottle of smelling salts, and twice in recent years, I have had to revive either a bride or a groom.

Prior to one large church wedding, the bride said to the groom, "You must say those vows out loud so everyone can hear you!"

When we reached the point where the groom was to repeat after me, "With this ring, I thee wed," he said, "With this wing, I thee red."

On a recent airplane flight, just as we were pulling away from the ramp, I noticed that the woman beside me had gripped the armrest so tightly that her knuckles were white. I knew I was in for an interesting flight.

Initially, I tried to ignore her anxiety. But when she began to cower against the seat, I decided it was my duty to at least talk to her in an effort to divert her attention. I discovered she had been in a nearly fatal plane wreck only a few months before and was not yet over her fear of flying. She had no choice but to make this plane trip, and she was absolutely terrified. During the entire flight, she gripped the armrest, shrank into the seat, and talked constantly about how frightened she was. It was a terrifying experience for her, and only a little less so for me. Her fear had destroyed her faith in the plane and in the pilot's ability.

Yes, fear can demolish our faith in countless ways, but it also can stimulate it. Our fear that we might use up all the fuel sources of the world has prompted us to believe we can solve the energy problem. Our fear that we may pollute the water, devastate the forests, and rob the earth of its natural resources has activated our belief that we can conserve those resources. Our fear that humanity may self-destruct in nuclear fratricide has aroused our belief that people of every race, nationality, and clime can live together in peace.

In addition, we should not overlook the fact that fear can serve as a stimulus to reactivate our own personal religious faith. The fear that we may miss the glory of life, its meaning and purpose, its abundance and joy, prompts us to find a renewed faith in God, in the salvational act of Jesus Christ, and in the saving fellowship of the church. The biblical injunction, "The fear of the Lord is the beginning of wisdom," is telling us that fear can be, and often is, an incentive in the development of faith.

In attempting to deal with fear, it is of the utmost importance to remember that fear can be overcome by love. The writer of I John says, "Perfect love casts out fear" (4:18). And the writer of II Timothy alluded to the same idea: "God hath not given us the spirit of fear; but of power, and of love, and of a sound mind" (1:7).

The fact that love can overcome fear is most quickly grasped when we realize that love and fear cannot live together in the same heart. Either the fear casts out love or the love drives out fear. Fear and love simply cannot coexist. Sophocles was aware of this: "Yet one little word makes all these toils as nought" (*Oedipus at Colonus,* line 1616). Love and fear cannot possibly dwell together.

Many times fear is caused by impatience, but love is patient. Fear is often caused by rejection, but love never rejects. Frequently, fear is caused by being overly demanding, but love never demands. Fear can be caused by doubt, but love never doubts. Therefore love drives fear out of our hearts.

The Center for Attitudinal Healing in California was begun in 1975 by a medical doctor who came to understand that some healing is the result of attitude—primarily, the attitude of love. A colleague related the following incident to me. A teenage boy had been injured in a tractor accident. He was blinded, permanently paralyzed except for one arm, and so consumed by fear he could not speak. There was no organic reason for his inability to speak; it was simply the result of fear. His mother took him to the Center, but he did not respond to treatment.

Then one day his mother noticed a two-year-old brain-damaged baby who cried pitifully nearly all the time. In a moment of inspiration, the boy's mother laid the baby beside her teenage son. At first, the boy was unwilling to even touch the baby. Finally, he began to pat the baby with his one hand, then stroked it, and soon the baby stopped crying. After a few days, the relationship between the teenage boy and the baby was so strong the boy was able to talk again; his fear had been cast out by love.

That's what love can do—it can drive out our fears. We should fill ourselves with love, overflowing, brimming full, until there is no room for fear. When we do that, love enlarges itself until it occupies all the available space in our hearts, minds, and souls, so there is no room for fear.

For you, for me, for all of us who have any fear—it is my hope that God will fill us with love, the love so perfectly revealed in his son, Jesus Christ; may we be so filled with love that it overflows in its abundance until there is no room for fear. Then we will experience the truth of the words "Perfect love casts out fear."

MARK 10:35-45
LUKE 19:1-10

Inferiority. An amazing aspect of the Bible is
that it speaks to every facet of our human predicament. Each of our strengths and weaknesses is not only
accurately diagnosed, but is also prescribed for in the
pages of the Bible. And after two thousand years of
study and the development of sophisticated intellec-
tual disciplines designed to diagnose and cure our
human frailties, little has been added to the insights
and understandings already present in this remarkable Book.

Inferiority is one of the human weaknesses
pinpointed in Scripture, and it is a major problem
today. It is estimated that 95 percent of us suffer to
some extent from a sense of personal unworthiness.
Perhaps some people do not recognize their problem,
but millions of us are handicapped in our quest for
happiness and success because we feel substandard.

It is true, of course, that every person is inferior to
someone else in some way. I can't play football as Tony
Dorsett does, or shoot a basket as well as Moses
Malone. I cannot write like Neil Simon, nor can I

dance as well as Mikhail Baryshnikov. I am inferior to all those people in some respects. No matter who or where we are, we can find someone to whom we feel inferior. We can find a better lawyer or a better doctor or a better secretary or a better cook. We can find someone with a larger bank account or with more influence or social standing.

While intellectually we recognize this phase of our humanity and realize we should accept it matter-of-factly, our problem is in our tendency to evaluate ourselves on the basis of comparison. And when we do that, we develop a sense of inferiority, because we almost always come out second-best. Then, having convinced ourselves we are also-rans, we decide we are not worthy, that we do not deserve to enjoy happiness or achieve success. Unfortunately, it then follows that we are prevented from expressing, without apology or guilt, the abilities and talents we do have.

This is the way it works: I discover I cannot preach as well as Dr. X. This leads me to feel unworthy to try to preach at all. That feeling of unworthiness prevents me from using those abilities and talents I do have, and I develop a deep sense of inferiority. Next, I am tempted either to give up entirely or to strive for a false sense of superiority, in which I convince myself I really am better than Dr. X. This is a superiority I cannot achieve, and my futile attempts to attain it make me utterly miserable. The harder I try, the more wretched I become. Therefore, my sense of inferiority eventually becomes a destructive force which handicaps my best self.

A healing response to our feeling of unworthiness is to understand that we are neither inferior nor superior. The truth is, I am simply me, and you are simply you. You are not in competition with anyone else, because there is no one else like you. You are unique—one of a kind. God did not make anyone else like you. You are not supposed to be like any other person; you couldn't be if you tried. And other people are not supposed to be like you; they couldn't be if they tried.

The Bible assists us at this point. First, there is the story about James and John, the sons of Zebedee who came to Jesus and said, "When you come into your kingdom, we want to sit at your left and right hand."

Our first response is, "How full of themselves they are! What superiority complexes! They're egomaniacs, to think they could sit that close to Jesus." However, our arm-chair psychological diagnosis is wrong, because James and John are actually revealing a deep sense of inferiority. They are so insecure, so unsure of themselves, that they must have the compliment, the security, of sitting at the right and the left of Jesus.

My father knew more about human nature than any other person I have ever known. Once when he was visiting us, a friend dropped by for a few minutes. My friend was rather cocky and boastful, and when he had left, my father said to me, "Son, be good to that man. He has a deep sense of inferiority."

In a similar manner, James and John were covering up their inner insecurity, their low self-esteem, their unwillingness to accept themselves for who they were. Their request is as revealing as the words of the little boy who said to his father, "Let's play darts, Daddy. I'll throw, and you say 'Wonderful!' "

That's what James and John were saying—"If we can sit at his right and left hand, then everyone will say, 'Look at James and John, they're wonderful!' "

For further help from the Bible, let's look at Zacchaeus, the short fellow who climbed the tree to see Jesus. If you read that story in depth, you will discover that Zacchaeus, too, had a terrific sense of inferiority. Some might feel he had good reason to deem himself inadequate. In the first place, he felt inferior because of his height. And he felt inferior because he was a tax collector. At that time, tax collectors were despised by the other townspeople, who criticized and condemned them. Nobody stroked him; nobody complimented him; no one said anything nice about him at all. Zacchaeus, in all probability, became overly defensive and perhaps even paranoid, thinking, "Everybody's out to get me just because I'm a tax collector." Once he had convinced himself he was unacceptable to others, it was easy to become unacceptable to himself.

In this frame of mind, Zacchaeus did what many of us do. He covered up his inferiority with a cockiness, a sense of superiority. One day he climbed a tree. How many of us use similar devices to conceal our inferiority? We climb the trees of social status, prestige, wealth, or professional recognition. We try to disguise our sense of inferiority by climbing any number of trees. However, these attempts are as useless to us as Zacchaeus' attempts were to him. Because, you see, once he clambered up the tree, he felt more inferior than ever because that emphasized his need to climb it. Zacchaeus was in need of help, and so are we.

Zacchaeus' predicament reminds me of a cartoon I saw recently. A man was sitting in a psychiatrist's office, and the psychiatrist was saying, "Sir, you not only feel inferior, you *are* inferior."

Zacchaeus was probably thinking to himself, "I don't just feel inferior; I actually *am* inferior."

As bleak as life may have looked to Zacchaeus, remember what happened. First of all, Jesus accepted him. Miracle of miracles, this short man, this despised tax collector, this thief, was recognized by Jesus: "Zacchaeus, I'm coming to your house for dinner tonight." He didn't say, "You'll have to repent before I'll come" or "You'll have to quit stealing before I'll come" or "You'll have to grow another twelve inches before I'll come." Jesus was saying, "Just as you are, Zacchaeus, I'm coming to dinner. I accept you."

An invitation is an affirmation, is it not? When someone invites you to do something, that's a way of saying, "You're accepted; I want to be with you. I like you. You're O.K." Zacchaeus must have felt astonishment and a deep joy that Jesus wanted to have dinner with him, no strings attached. That enhanced his self-esteem, which in turn induced an inner security and a self-assurance that destroyed his need to wear a mask. Each one of us needs to be accepted by somebody.

Our common need for acceptance is illustrated in the fairy tale *Rapunzel*. You may remember that it is about a beautiful young woman who was imprisoned in a tower by a witch. The witch had convinced the lovely girl that she was in truth ugly, and the girl believed her—until one day she saw Prince Charming at the foot of the tower. She threw her golden tresses out the tower window. They fell to the ground, where Prince Charming braided them into a ladder and climbed up to rescue her. When she saw the adoration in his eyes, she knew she was not ugly. His love and acceptance freed her—not just from the confinement of the tower, but from the tyranny of her own sense of inferiority.

Someone must come along and say to us, "You're accepted." We need the affirmation of others; we need it as desperately as did the imprisoned Rapunzel.

The affirmation of others will, in turn, enable us to accept ourselves, just as Jesus' affirmation of Zacchaeus enabled him to accept himself. "If Jesus could accept me," Zacchaeus must have thought, "I can accept myself." Then he no longer needed to climb trees or wear masks or be overly defensive. He could let go of his self-pity, his jealousy, his envy, and his feeling of inferiority. How marvelous that must have been. Zacchaeus must have felt free.

Now he could say, "Hey world, I'm Zacchaeus! I hope you like me; I want you to like me. But if you don't, it's O.K., because I've accepted myself."

A similar freedom would be wonderful for all of us. All Christians should have the inner security that enables us to say, "It's me. I hope you like me; I want you to like me. But if you don't, it's O.K., because I accept myself." Self-acceptance is necessary if we are to overcome a sense of inferiority.

Another reason for the necessity of such self-acceptance is that our self-image dictates our conduct. Whether we know it or not, we act out our self-image in our daily behavior. If our self-image is bad, we act that out; if it's good, we act that out.

In *Windows, Ladders, and Bridges*, Dr. A. Dudley Dennison made that principle very clear in a story about author A. J. Cronin, who was also a physician.

When Cronin was in medical school, one of his professors told him his performance in surgery was unacceptable. He might possibly become a general practitioner, but never a surgeon. When Cronin finished medical school, he went to a remote area in the Scottish highlands to practice medicine. He was the only physician within hundreds of miles.

One winter there was a terrible snow storm. During the height of the blizzard a huge tree fell on the son of the local pastor, crushing his spine. Dr. Cronin realized that without a delicate neurological operation, the boy might be permanently paralyzed. But he was afraid to try because he was acting out the image his professor had of him—that he was a terrible surgeon. That kept ringing in his ears while the boy's father begged him to operate.

"But then something happened," Cronin said. "For the first time, I questioned the validity of that man's verdict. . . . Doubts and fears swept away. I knew I could operate successfully. And with God's help I did" ([Zondervan, 1976], p. 181).

We all live out our self-image in our daily conduct. A poet once expressed it this way:

> God loves me here and now;
> His hand's in everything.
> . . . .
>
> I love myself as God does,
> And I can celebrate.
> —Anonymous

Let us think of Zacchaeus again. Once he could accept himself, he was able to accept others. If we intend to handle our sense of inferiority, we not only must be accepted and accept ourselves, we also must accept others. However, accepting others must *follow* accepting ourselves, because we cannot forgive others until we have forgiven ourselves; we cannot love others until we have learned to love ourselves. Theologian Paul Tillich said that only those who are able to love themselves can love others; only those who have overcome self-contempt can overcome their contempt of others.

This is indeed true. Many studies have proved beyond a shadow of a doubt that there is definite correlation between self-acceptance and accepting others. The person with a low level of self-acceptance has scant ability to accept others. So Zacchaeus could now accept himself; he no longer felt inferior; and he could accept others—including his accusers and his critics.

Zacchaeus' growth continued as he became the person God intended him to be. Freed now from the sense of inferiority that had been destroying him, Zacchaeus could say, "Lord, I repent. I'm sorry. I ask forgiveness, and I want to restore fourfold to all those from whom I wrongly have taken." To everyone from whom he had stolen a dollar, he gave back four. He accepted the possibility God had intended for him—to be God's man, a man of faith. He accepted the forgiveness of God and the gift of salvation God offered to him in Jesus Christ. The Scripture doesn't tell us, but it is safe to assume that Zacchaeus became a follower of Jesus Christ and a witness to God's saving word.

I can imagine that in the years until his death, whenever Zacchaeus saw a stranger, he would say, "Let me tell you what happened to me. I was insecure, with a low self-esteem, a sense of inferiority, wishing I could be somebody else, miserable on the inside. And then Jesus came and touched my life. He accepted me unconditionally and loved me. That enabled me to accept myself and to accept others and to become God's man. This is who I am now. O happy day! I am free of the damnable sense of inferiority that threatened to destroy my life."

During pre-Civil War days in New Orleans, some slaves—spiritless, despairing, hopeless—were working. But among them, one man stood with his head erect and his spirit unbroken.

Someone asked, "Who is that fellow? Is he the straw boss, or perhaps the owner of the slaves?"

"No," the reply came. "That fellow can't get it out of his head that he is the son of a king."

That's the good news. You are not inferior! You are the son or the daughter of a King!

JOHN 16:32

Loneliness.

The song "Eleanor Rigby" has a haunting melody and an insightful message. At various times in our lives each of us can identify with that melancholy young lady, because Eleanor Rigby, according to the song, is very lonely. She sits by the window and waits for someone to come. Looking out the window, she hopes, prays, and wishes that somebody, anybody, will come. But nobody comes because no one cares. When Eleanor Rigby dies, Father McKenzie prepares her funeral sermon and delivers it, but nobody comes, nobody cares. Then the refrain: "Ah, look at all the lonely people."

This is an accurate commentary on our day. There is a deep-seated, profound loneliness in our urbanized, impersonal society. We are told that 75 to 90 percent of all the people in America suffer from some degree of chronic loneliness and that the malaise is spreading rapidly. Loneliness hurts deeply, and its physical, mental, and spiritual effects are terrifying.

Now, some may try to define loneliness as merely a separation from people, but that definition is far too simplistic to describe the aching isolation. One can be lonely in a crowd. Being apart from people is not the loneliness that darkens our lives. I well remember feeling very lonely while standing in Times Square amid thousands. Being away from people is not loneliness.

In a "Peanuts" cartoon, Sophie said to Lucy, "I'm lonesome and I want to go home."

"How can you be lonesome in a place so full of kids?" Lucy asked. "How could you possibly be lonesome in a place where there's so much to do?"

And Sophie replied, "The more you talk, the more lonesome I get." Being with a crowd of people or hearing lots of conversation seldom dispels loneliness.

The loneliness we feel can come to us in various ways. It can come at a time of sorrow, when someone we love is separated from us. Santayana captured this feeling in "With You a Part of Me":

> With you a part of me hath passed away;
> . . . .
> And I am grown much older in a day.
> . . . .
> I scarce know which part may greater be—
> What I keep of you, or you rob from me.
> —*Poems*

Some of us experience this deep, unmanageable sense of loneliness when someone has been taken from us by death.

Loneliness may come to those who would like to be married, but are not, through no fault of their own. Sometimes, if the isolation is felt deeply enough, such lonely people go to desperate lengths.

For instance, a Dallas man recently ran a newspaper advertisement: "I want a wife. I want a wife immediately. I'm talking about marriage." A beautiful young woman who worked at a car rental company answered the ad the first day it ran. The next day the two of them had lunch together, that night they had dinner, and the next morning they were married and went to Las Vegas for their honeymoon. I'm reluctant to criticize, because I have some understanding of the profound sense of loneliness that would compel two persons to join themselves in marriage even though they do not really know each other.

Loneliness sometimes comes to those who are in the sunset years of life. There are millions of people in America today in rest homes, nursing centers, and retirement communities who feel a deep sense of loneliness. They have no work to do; therefore, there is seemingly no purpose to their lives, no meaning. They're separated from those they love and those who love them. Like the psalmist, they are tempted to say, "I look to the right and watch, but there is none who takes notice of me; no refuge remains to me, no man cares for me" (142:4 RSV).

Loneliness also can stem from responsibility. Think of the lone breadwinner who must feed children, clothe them, provide for their education. Sometimes the wage earner is a male, sometimes a female. Both men and women can suffer the great sense of loneliness that comes from this obligation. There are also individuals who occupy positions of responsibility and are faced daily with decisions. The buck stops with them. They close their doors and pray that God will help them make the right decisions. That's a terrifying loneliness.

Loneliness sometimes comes from having to stand

up for your convictions against the prevailing mood and temper of the time. All of us have had that experience to one degree or another. Then our loneliness is fed by separation from those we thought were our friends, but who now reject us because we have opinions with which they do not agree.

Whatever the source of our loneliness, regretfully, no one can possibly know exactly how we feel. In times past I have said to people, "I know how you feel; I've lost a loved one, too" or "I know how you feel; I've gone through a similar experience." I no longer say that, because no one can possibly know how another feels.

Loneliness and love are like two sides of the same coin. We cannot split the coin to keep the love and eliminate the loneliness. We cannot even share the loneliness. No one else knows how we feel. Thomas Wolfe wrote some tragic letters about loneliness to his friend Aline Bernstein. He wrote of moments when he felt he would commit suicide, so deep and horrible was his sense of aloneness. Despite an unusually lucid and detailed description of his pain, she was never able to really understand how he could feel so alone.

When loneliness overcomes us, no one can share it with us completely. We feel like Elijah under the juniper tree: "I, even I only, am left." In the counseling study I have dealt with persons who have felt like that—"I, even I only, am left."

What does the Christian faith have to say about this? What does it have to offer the millions of people who suffer from loneliness? To answer that question, we should understand that loneliness is caused by a lack of security, by being out of contact with meaningful love. The Christian faith allows us to reestablish the security of a loving relationship, both internally and externally, and to claim or rebuild a support system that enables us to defeat our loneliness, or at least to bear it.

You see, each of us needs an external support system. It is absolutely necessary that we have some kind of support, be it one person or a group. It may be a husband or a wife or a friend, it may be a small group, but there must be someone (or something) upon whom we can lean. A support system must accept us as we are, nonjudgmentally and unconditionally—ask no questions, pronounce no judgments, offer no criticisms. Not many of us have someone who gives us that kind of support. Ask yourself how many persons in the world could accept you just as you are right now, without asking any questions or offering any criticism whatsoever. There are probably very few, and that is what makes our support systems so tenuous.

In the movie *Looking for Mr. Goodbar,* one woman asks another for a very great favor. The second responds nonjudgmentally and grants the favor. The first woman thanks her and says, "Everybody in the world needs just one person who won't ever blame them." We should have just one person who never blames, never accuses, never criticizes, never pronounces judgment.

When I was about ten or eleven, I went bicycle riding with a group of friends one day. After a while, we became bored and decided to perform tricks on our bicycles. Each stunt we were able to do made us brave enough to try another; I decided I was good enough to stand on the seat and ride without holding on. My acrobatic attempt resulted in a broken arm.

When my friends took me home, my parents, thank goodness, weren't there.

I lay on the couch in great pain, but the broken bone did not bother me nearly as much as the dread of having to tell my parents how it happened. I knew I would get a lecture, a sermon. I deserved it, but I dreaded it. It was a freeing, wonderful experience when my parents were insightful enough to know I had already pronounced judgment upon myself. They did not lecture, condemn, or criticize. They accepted my error with nonjudgmental love. It is necessary for all of us to have such external support in order to handle our loneliness.

But surprisingly enough, external support systems are not limited to people. They may be *places* of renewal—a field, a forest, an inner sanctum, the experience of worship, the fellowship of a church— where our batteries can be recharged, our energies refueled, our spirits reinforced, our enthusiasm revived. One of my favorite people says she cannot sleep on Saturday night in anticipation of the excitement of going to church on Sunday morning. She has found, in the experience of worship and in church groups, a support system that surrounds her with a network of love. She needs this support system, and she is wise enough to value it.

An external support system also may be obtained through learning to help others. There once was a highly successful businessman named Bill. He was intelligent and competitive, but he was also very lonely in his position of responsibility. He became an alcoholic. After much effort, he was able to conquer his drinking habit—at least for a while.

Then he went on a business trip to Akron, Ohio, and, while there, had too much free time. He became obsessed with the notion that he had to have a drink, but he knew if he had one, he would have two, and then another. The idea came to him that perhaps the answer to his loneliness, and therefore to his obsession with drink, would be to help someone else. He asked around until he found ten other alcoholics. He called them together in his hotel and they began to help one another. In that group was a man named Dr. Bob, and out of that experience, Bill and Dr. Bob formed Alcoholics Anonymous. These men have proved that helping somebody else is a valid part of our external support system.

Yet, by itself, an *external* support system is not sufficient. We must also have an *internal* support system. There must be peace, calm, and serenity within us; we must have a sense of the presence of the Divine Companion. Jesus promised: "Lo, I am with you alway, even unto the end of the world" (Matt. 28:20).

Epictetus wrote, "When then you have shut the doors and made darkness within, remember never to say that you are alone, for you are not; but God is within" (*Discourses,* Bk. 1. 14). We are never ever alone, because the presence of the Divine Companion, the Holy Spirit, is always within us. "Thou wilt keep him in perfect peace, whose mind is stayed on thee" (Isa. 26:3). "The eternal God is thy refuge, and underneath are the everlasting arms" (Deut. 33:27).

A well-known minister was once afflicted with a deep sense of loneliness. He could not explain its origin and he could not overcome it. Soon his loneliness drove him into a depression he could not handle. One day as he sat in his living room, some words suddenly flashed through his mind. Those words are found in John's Gospel. There Jesus says, "He who sent me is with me. He has not left me alone" (8:28). At once the minister's loneliness began to recede and he found a new sense of the Divine Presence within himself. He often recalled those words in the days and years that followed—"He who sent me is with me. He has not left me alone"—and they became the internal support system he needed to combat his loneliness.

The internal security each of us needs is provided by our faith. We must make the leap of faith that allows us to live successfully with the questions in our lives. You see, we want answers when we are lonely. Many times in the counseling study, I have dealt with persons experiencing the pain of deep loneliness.

They say, "Tell me why. I want to know why. Explain it to me."

But faith says, "Don't ask for answers; live with the questions." Then we can live peacefully with our loneliness in the knowledge that we cannot explain it, that there are no satisfactory answers for the untimely death of a loved one, the fact that we have not found a life partner, or must bear burdensome responsibilities. Our faith allows us to live serenely and happily with our loneliness.

In her *Letters to a Young Poet,* Rainer Maria Rilke counseled: "Be patient toward all that is unsolved in your heart and try to love the *questions themselves.* . . . Do not now seek the answers, which cannot be given you because you would not be able to live them. And the point is, to live everything. *Live* the questions now. Perhaps you will then gradually, without noticing it, live along some distant day into the answer" ([W. W. Norton, 1954], p. 35).

Faith is the willingness to commit the answers to the future, and the future to God. This enables us to live with the questions today. Faith is to be able to say with the Apostle, "I know whom I have believed, and am persuaded that he is able to keep that which I have committed unto him against that day" (II Tim. 1:12*b*). It is to understand the last verse of William Cullen Bryant's poem:

> He who, from zone to zone,
> Guides through the boundless sky thy certain flight,
> In the long way that I must tread alone,
> Will lead my steps aright.
>
> —"To a Waterfowl"

This is a part of the internal support system that enables us to deal with our loneliness.

When Rupert Brooke was beginning a long sea voyage, there was no one to see him off. He left the ship, walked down on the pier, and found a dirty, ragged little boy who said his name was William. Mr. Brooke offered the child sixpence if he would wave good-bye to him. William said he would. The last thing Rupert Brooke saw in the distance as the ship departed was a ragged little boy with a white handkerchief—almost white—waving good-bye. He said he had received his sixpence worth and his farewell, and he did not feel lonely anymore.

For the Christian, it does not even cost sixpence. For when we are lonely, there is always One who stands on the pier of life to offer security, acceptance, and love to each one who feels all alone and lonely.

PSALM 130
II CORINTHIANS 1:8

Depression. Although it may come as a shock

to some people, the saints were totally human. And we are fortunate they were, because their humanness is precisely what makes their lives so instructive for you and me. The saints suffered the same frailties, the same temptations, as you and I.

Paul is a case in point. In Second Corinthians, he tells about the devastating blow he received in Asia: "We were so utterly, unbearably crushed that we despaired of life itself. Why, we felt that we had received the sentence of death" (1:8b-9 RSV). Obviously, Paul was discouraged, disappointed, and depressed by that experience. The writer of Psalm 130 was also depressed: "Out of the depths I cry unto thee, O Lord." He, too, felt demoralized.

Some of the great saints of our own day also have suffered from depression. The marvelous Christian missionary and mystic E. Stanley Jones was so disheartened early in his missionary life that he was on the verge of a nervous breakdown. He thought he could not go on. Leslie Weatherhead, a famous

London preacher, suffered at times from serious depression. And, as so many students of American history are aware, Abraham Lincoln was sometimes so dispirited he entertained visions of lying in his own coffin.

The great statesman and leader Winston Churchill was a victim of prolonged periods of depression. Among a multitude of other concerns, he always worried about his health. His doctor said that Churchill was forever gargling something; at the back of his mind there constantly lurked the suspicion that he might have pneumonia. He was haunted by his political failures, remembering his own father, who had been relegated to political obscurity at an early age. When Winston was unceremoniously defeated by the British electorate in 1945, he was very despondent. He would never stand at the rail of a ship or at the edge of a train platform; he was afraid "a few drops of desperation" might seize him and he would jump. He even had a name for his depression—"black dog."

Are there any of us who do not know that black dog? Is there a human being who has not known at least a temporary paralysis of depression that prevents normal physical, mental, and spiritual functioning? There are varying degrees of depression, of course, but I suspect each of us is familiar with our own personal black dog.

In *Pilgrim's Progress,* the Slough of Despond is a deep quagmire all Christians must cross. Each person must, sooner or later, in one degree or another, cross the Slough of Despond, that perilous morass of the black dog. At such times, what does the Christian faith tell us to do?

First of all, the psalmist helps by suggesting that when we are depressed, we need to talk it out. That's what the psalmist did: "Out of the depths I cry to thee, O LORD! Lord, hear my voice! Let thy ears be attentive to the voice of my supplications!" (130:1-2 RSV). The apostle Paul also talked out his distress with God. Relief comes with the verbalization of our feelings. When we are depressed we need to talk it out with God, and also with someone who is able to listen and is empathetic enough to identify with our problems.

Winston Churchill was blessed with a wife who was sensitive to his prolonged depressions and knew how to listen and identify nonjudgmentally. Putting our dejection into words often reveals it in its proper perspective and releases heretofore blocked energies.

Articulating our depression also helps us to identify its causes. When we identify the grounds for our depression, we are better able to deal with it. But we tend to focus on the effects of our depression rather than on its causes. We zero in on our listlessness, lifelessness, loss of appetite, lack of sleep. We are wasting time and energy when we examine the effects rather than trying to identify the cause.

We find it difficult to identify the cause of our depression because we are totally subjective. We can never be objective about ourselves. That is why it's so important to have someone else to talk to. We can receive an objective viewpoint; we can, so to speak, look in a mirror to find the cause. When we try to heal our own illness, overcome our own humanity, cure our own depression, we usually fail because our subjectivity reveals only effects, and we cannot overcome our depression without dealing with the causes.

A prevailing theory proposes that some depression is caused by the absence of a chemical in the body that creates a certain response in the brain cells. I believe that is valid, and medication is now available for that physical condition.

On the other hand, depression can also be caused by grief, guilt, failure, rejection, loneliness, fear, stress. Some thinking indicates that much depression is caused by anger, an anger we cannot admit or express directly, an inverted anger. There is certainly some degree of truth in that belief.

Whatever its cause, we need to deal with our depression with objectivity, with honesty; often we need to deal with it through confession, repentance, and the acceptance of forgiveness. We need to cleanse the interior of our soul in an attempt to eliminate the cause of our depression.

We also need to learn to count our blessings. Research has shown that when we think pleasant thoughts—that is, when we count our blessings—we are better able to see, taste, smell, hear, and even detect finer differences in touch. Eyesight improves immediately, memory is improved, and the mind is more relaxed.

That's not so strange, is it? Four thousand years ago King Solomon said, "A merry heart doeth good like a medicine, but a broken spirit drieth up like bones." Counting our blessings is an antidote for depression.

In response to this suggestion, I've heard people say, "I just can't think of my blessings because I've got so many problems. I'm so depressed. I just can't help it." Ah, but you can help it; you have the choice. You can count your blessings, or you can count your problems.

Have you ever been in the studio audience for the filming of a television show? As a rule, someone will come out and hold up a sign: APPLAUSE. There may not be anything to applaud, but everybody responds with an ovation. In a little while, someone comes out and holds up another sign: LAUGHTER. There may not be anything funny at all, but everybody laughs. The audience responds very much like a roomful of robots. And that's exactly what we do in life. Some circumstance of life says, "Be depressed," and we're depressed. Another event says, "Be discouraged," and so we are discouraged. Like robots, we respond to the negative signs that are flashed before us. But we should not do so! We can ignore those signs and choose instead to count our blessings.

That's not deluding ourselves, nor is it being dishonest, because our blessings are just as real as our problems. It's a matter of deciding where we will place the emphasis. It is just as easy, just as honest, and just as authentic to choose to count our blessings as to choose to count our problems. An old gospel hymn reminds us of this truth:

When upon life's billows you are tempest tossed,
When you are discouraged, thinking all is lost,
Count your many blessings, name them one by one,
And it will surprise you what the Lord hath done.

Count your blessings. That's what Paul did; that's what the psalmist did. After he cried out unto the Lord, the psalmist began to talk about hope and waiting and the presence of God. That's also what the saints did—they counted their blessings. And that's what scores of other people throughout the ages have done. When they felt depressed, they counted their blessings and found it an effective remedy.

When we are afflicted with black dog, we also need to learn to hang on a little longer. The well-known preacher Dr. Raymond Balcomb was three years old when his father was killed in a tragic automobile accident. His mother was left with a house full of children—before the days of Social Security. She had to work from early morning until late in the evening just to provide the necessities of life. When those burdens became too heavy and the odds seemed overwhelming, she would say, "When you get to the end of your rope, tie a knot and hang on."

This is excellent advice. When the odds are overwhelmingly against you, when you are afraid you're about to be thrown off the merry-go-round of life, when you come to the end of your rope, just tie a knot and hang on. Robert Louis Stevenson was not unaquainted with the problem of depression. He was ill most of his life and seldom lived a day without pain, yet he said, "Every man can get through until nightfall." And indeed we can, if we tie a knot and hang on.

"This too shall pass" is one of my favorite adages. Black dog always passes. It may come again another day, but if we tie a knot and hang on, it will pass.

It helps enormously if we will do something for someone else when we're depressed. That has been my personal experience. When I am really depressed, I seek help by finding somebody for whom I can do something. That gets our minds off our own problems and shifts the focus from self to others. After all, depression, like our other human frailties, is partially caused by a preoccupation with ourselves and our own needs. When we go out and lose our lives in helping others, we also benefit.

In *A Touch of Wonder*, Arthur Gordon tells about a woman who had every good reason to be depressed and often was. He asked what she did when her depression seemed to be getting the better of her. She replied that she picked a bunch of flowers and found a shut-in to give them to, or found something else she could do for someone.

Finally, in order to combat depression, turn to God. When you have black dog, when you're dispirited, turn to God. Paul turned to God. He said the experience in Asia made "us rely not on ourselves but on God who raises the dead" (II Cor. 1:9*b* RSV). Think about it. God has kept you safe in the past; he will keep you safe in the future.

Rufus Jones, one of the great Christians of an earlier generation, was saddled with chronic depression. His biographer said that Jones' faith in God enabled him to live above the level of his moods. That's what trust in God does—it enables us to live above the level of our moods.

Once a group of botanists was on an expedition in Scotland. In a tiny crevice on a steep cliff, they discovered a rare flower they wanted to retrieve but could not reach. Then they noticed a shepherd and his son nearby. They asked the little boy if he would allow them to tie a rope around his waist and lower him down the side of the cliff to retrieve the rare flower.

After a moment of hesitation, the little boy said, "I'll do it if you let my father hold the rope."

All of us need to remember to turn to God, trust him, and let him hold the rope.

II CORINTHIANS 12:7-10

Failure.

Today millions of us are being victimized by what might be called the success syndrome. The pressure upon Americans to succeed is both tremendous in its scope and tragic in its consequences. Children and teenagers, as well as adults, are under unbelievable pressure. Winning is everything, and we view failure as the worst thing that can happen. This drive to succeed, combined with the fear of failure, becomes a dual problem.

Yet because we're only human, all of us do fail at one time or another. We fail in school, in business, in our marriages, in our homes, in our families, or in our health. Failure is a universal experience. It comes to everyone sooner or later. Even if we do our best, we sometimes fail. And if our goals are too low, we have failed in nerve and courage.

Countless people are asking how they can handle their failure. Tolstoy, in his *Confessions,* suggested that most individuals respond in one of four ways: They become frightened and get drunk; they despair and commit suicide; they resent their failure and harden their hearts against it; or they accept it and grin and bear it. Our reactions to failure are doubtless as varied as our personalities.

An interesting result of the prevalence of failure is the large number of enterprising "experts" who try to figure out ways to eliminate failure, rather than allowing us to accept it as part of life. They offer courses, write books, and direct seminars that guarantee an immunity to failure.

Many persons in the Bible experienced failure. The apostle Paul was persecuted; he was rejected. He wanted very much to go to Spain, but found himself in a prison cell in Rome. He had a thorn in his flesh. We don't know what it was, but it was painful. He prayed that God would remove the thorn, but this did not happen. Yet Paul discovered an answer, for God spoke to him: "My grace is sufficient for you, for my strength is made perfect in weakness."

Jesus, too, experienced failure. On the cross he prayed, "My God, my God, why hast thou forsaken me?" But God's grace was sufficient to turn that failure into victory.

As Christians, how are we to handle failure? First, we should admit we have failed. That's what Paul did. He simply admitted it. This suggestion does not apply to those who only think they have failed; they are the neurotic victims of a lack of proper self-esteem. However, when healthy people fail, it's best to admit it—not with remorse or self-pity, but honestly and realistically.

The victories of life are won by those who are willing to admit they have failed. It is not a sin or a crime to fail, and failing does not mean we are failures. It is healthy and redemptive to admit it when we fail—not regretfully or morbidly, but openly, realistically. It is O.K. to fail, because that is part of our human predicament.

We also need to accept our failure. Please realize that it is possible to admit failure without accepting it. Paul had a problem with that acceptance until he understood God's answer. We, too, sometimes have problems accepting failure. We must remember that we are not alone; everyone experiences failure. It is one of the inevitables of living. Nonetheless, it is not always easy to accept.

When I was in the sixth grade, I played second base for our school softball team. We won every game that year and thus competed for the city championship. It was a big game. In the last half of the last inning the score was tied. The bases were loaded and two men were out. The batter hit a short fly ball just over my head. I ran as fast as I could. I leaped as high as I could. My glove touched the ball, but it caromed off for a hit. The runner scored and we lost the championship.

I readily admitted my failure, but I could not accept it. For weeks, I reran that play in my mind. If I had just started a little sooner, jumped a little higher, reached farther! I felt guilty. I felt shame and remorse. I kept telling myself, "I could have caught that ball! It's my fault; I lost the game. I failed."

On December 9, 1914, the vast Edison Industries burned to the ground. Thomas Edison was sixty-seven at that time; it was too late in life to begin again. As the fire raged, his son, then a young man, was heartbroken for his father. He found Edison standing near the blaze, his face ruddy in the glow, his white hair blown by the wind. Edison turned to his son and told him to find his mother. "Bring her here. She will never see anything like this again as long as she lives." That's what it means to accept failure. Admit it, accept it, and then use it. Failure is a great teacher.

I have had some successes and many failures, and I cannot think of one single lesson I have ever learned from accomplishment. Although I may have gained self-confidence, I've never learned anything from success. But, oh, what I've learned from failure! Most of what I know about people, about myself, and about my profession, I have learned from failure.

Carl Jung remarked that psychotherapists learn little or nothing from their successes; they mainly confirm mistakes. Their failures, on the other hand, are priceless experiences; they not only open the way to a deeper truth, but force a change in views and methods. To paraphrase Robert Hamilton's "Along the Road":

> I walked a mile with *Success.*
>   She chattered all the way,
> But left me none the wiser
>   For all she had to say.
>
> I walked a mile with *Failure,*
>   And ne'er a word said she;
> But, oh, the things I learned from her
>   When *Failure* walked with me.

In a course on failure offered at MIT, delineations of definitions—Failure-bad and Failure-learn—are used. Failure-bad refers to failure from which nothing is learned; Failure-learn is failure from which one profits. Learn from failure; use it as a teacher. The apostle Paul learned from his failures; they became not losing experiences, but learning experiences.

In addition, we can dedicate our failures. We can dedicate them to God, offer them up to him. This will give them an aura of sacredness. We are human; God made us that way. And because we are human, we fail; hence, God has a stake in our failures. So why not dedicate our failures to God just as freely as we dedicate our successes? Some time ago a businessman said to me, "I want to dedicate my achievements to God. I could never have accomplished what I have on my own. I owe it to God." Why not dedicate our failures also?

Several years ago a man told me, "I failed in my marriage. We both made a wholehearted effort. We sought counseling and help. We honestly did everything we could, but we failed. It's over. But now I am just beginning to realize how very much I gained through that failure. I learned maturity, wisdom, insight, understanding, compassion, and tolerance. I am so much richer because of my failure." And then he said, "Would it be all right if I dedicated my failure to God?"

I had never heard of that before, but I said, "Indeed, why not? Dedicate your failure to God."

As I thought about the man's question, I realized that Paul had done the same thing. His persecution, his shipwreck, his disappointment, his thorn in the flesh—all were dedicated to God.

The Gospel of Luke describes the crucifixion of Jesus Christ: "It was now about the sixth hour, and there was darkness over the whole land. . . . The curtain of the temple was torn in two. Then Jesus, crying with a loud voice, said, 'Father, into thy hands I commit my spirit!' And having said this, he breathed his last" (23:44, 45b-46 RSV). On the cross, Christ faced what appeared to be a dismal failure and dedicated it to God.

We too can dedicate our failures to God, thus making them a part of the sacred privilege of living the lives God gave us.

Finally, we should forget our failures, dismiss them from our minds. I know we can't make them disappear, but neither should they lurk on the conscious level.

In one of his books, Maxwell Maltz says that people pitching horseshoes for the first time will miss the stake more times than they will hit it. Logic indicates that if they keep repeating this, they will learn to miss more and more. But the fact is, they learn to hit the stake more often. Why is that? Because the computer of the brain remembers the successes and forgets the failures, thereby reinforcing the successful attempts.

Our brains will do that, but many people mentally nurture their failures; they force their brains to remember their failures and forget their successes. They impress their failures indelibly upon their conscious minds and constantly inflict themselves with shame and remorse so that their failures seem to grow while their successes diminish. But that's not the way God created us. God wants us to forget our failures.

You may remember that Paul had a lot of forgetting to do. He had been a persecutor of the Christians. He probably was present at the stoning of

Stephen. But he possessed insight: "Forgetting those things which are behind . . . I press toward the mark for the prize of the high calling of God in Christ Jesus" (Phil. 3:13*b*, 14). He knew he could not find victory in Christ as long as he was burdened with the weight of his failures. And so it is with us—no possibility of future success exists as long as we carry the burdens of our past failures.

It would have been impossible for Peter to preach that marvelous sermon at Pentecost where three thousand were added to the church, had he been carrying in his conscious mind the memory of his shameful denial of Jesus Christ. Indeed, we must forget our failures if we are to press forward to success in the future. God is not nearly as interested in our past failures as in our present direction. He is not much interested in where we have been, but very concerned about where we are going; not so much with the setting of our life as with the set of our life.

How should we handle our failures? We should admit them, accept them, use them to learn, dedicate them to God, and then forget them. And we should hear the word of the Lord—"My grace is sufficient for you" (II Cor. 12:9 RSV).

ISAIAH 5:1-7
PHILIPPIANS 3:12-21
MATTHEW 21:33-43

Rejection.

Rejection. Many men and women whose stories are recounted in the Bible suffered the harsh experience of personal rejection. The Old Testament prophets—Elijah, Jeremiah, Amos, Hosea—all felt the anguish of being rejected. Paul also knew this ache, and in some instances, it was especially painful because he was rejected by those he most wanted to win.

Jesus himself was rejected—abused by his enemies, who crucified him; repudiated by a friend, who betrayed him; disclaimed by a disciple, who denied him. The words in Second Isaiah accurately describe Jesus: "He was despised and rejected by men." It is the human predicament to be cast off, excluded. We are rejected by strangers as well as by those we know. Sometimes we are rejected by friends, family, loved ones. At times we feel rejected even by God himself. Whatever the source, most of us know the painful experience of rejection. It cuts across the soul like a dull knife and leaves a jagged wound that is slow to heal.

We will do almost anything to avoid rejection. Nor do we like to talk about it; it is embarrassing to admit we have been rejected. We forget that this is an experience common to all of us.

My first memory of rejection goes back to the fifth grade when I fell passionately in love. She was a beautiful brunette, absolutely irresistible. I felt the stomach queasiness that is sometimes symptomatic of love. I wanted so much to be able to talk to her, to hold her hand. Finally, after several weeks, I worked up the courage to ask her if I could walk her home from school one day. She said no. Furthermore, despite my inexperience and youthful optimism, I was keenly aware that it was an unyielding no. I can still recall the devastation and destructiveness of that rejection.

Since then I have been rejected many times; sometimes it was real, at other times it was only imagined. But whether real or imagined, we need to remember that rejection happens to everyone; we are not alone. Because we are human we will suffer rejection. Therefore, let us turn our thoughts to what we can do about it.

First of all, we need to evaluate it. We must realize that rejection is related to our expectations. At times we may expect another person to accept us, and there are occasions when we expect a person to reject us. It is easy to think, "Oh, I know he won't like me" or "She won't think I'm good-looking" or "He'll think I'm ignorant" or "He won't accept me; I'm not in his social group." Negative expectation usually results in rejection.

Often our expectation is negative because we want to punish ourselves. Perhaps we want to prove ourselves worthless. Or we may want to feel guilty. Many people are not comfortable unless they feel guilty about something, and that attitude guarantees rejection.

Personally, I have a problem with cats. A girl I dated in college had a cat. That cat didn't like me, and every time I went in the girl's house, the cat would arch its back and hiss. Now when I see a cat, I expect it to reject me, and it usually does.

In order to combat our negative expectations we must learn to evaluate rejection. Is it real or is it imagined? Is it actual or just a feeling? Is it merely our expectation? Is it overt? Is it self-imposed? Is it self-rejection?

Jesus was rejected by the religious and political leaders of his day, and by his friends and disciples as well. That rejection was actual; it was real. On the cross, in a temporary moment of discouragement, Jesus cried, "My God, my God, why hast thou forsaken me?" But God had not forsaken him. His feeling of rejection was real, but the rejection was not.

We must evaluate our own rejections. Are they actual or only a feeling? Oftentimes we will need a confidante to help us make that evaluation, but it is important that we do so.

We should also remember that it is our response to rejection that really counts, not the rejection itself. Most of us overrespond to rejection by becoming angry or hostile, by withdrawing, by eating or drinking compulsively, or by experiencing the collapse of our self-esteem.

This letter appeared in an advice column recently: "The only man I ever loved ran away with another woman, and I have been depressed ever since.

I am a compulsive eater, and I am getting fat, and I never want to meet another man."

The counselor replied that the woman was responding to the rejection in the wrong way. Because of her fear of another rejection, she was escaping through overeating and withdrawal. She was told she needed to look at the positive side of life, rather than at the negative, and begin to respond with love and acceptance. That is excellent advice. The way we respond to rejection is important.

I once read about a boy who had applied to a university for admission and been rejected. He wrote the following letter:

> Dear Admissions Officer:
> I am in receipt of your rejection of my application. As much as I would like to accommodate you, I find that I cannot accept it. I have already received four rejections from other colleges and that number is, in fact, over my limit. Therefore, I must reject your rejection and, as much as this might inconvenience you, I expect to appear for classes on September 18.

I don't know whether that story is apocryphal or not, but knowing how to respond to rejection is of the utmost importance.

Let's look at the other side of the coin for a moment. Surprisingly enough, despite its distinctly negative connotations, rejection does have positive aspects. We can learn from it. For one thing, rejection often offers a clearer view of ourselves. After having been rejected, we should go off in a corner and take a good hard look at ourselves. Rejection reduces us to life-size; it purifies us of our pretensions, our affectations, our vanities, our selfishness. It does enable us to see ourselves more objectively.

There is another positive aspect of rejection. It teaches us that vulnerability to the pain of rejection is the price we pay for loving. The pain is minimal if someone we don't care about rejects us. But when someone we care for very much rejects us, the pain is intense. That's why lovers, parents, and children feel the pain of rejection so acutely. Those who love deeply will feel the pain of rejection most deeply. But to really live, we must really love, so the pain is worth it.

Jesus experienced the pain of rejection more intensely because he loved more profoundly. Only by giving his life to others could he bring life to them. But in so doing he exposed himself to the hurt and pain of rejection, and so it is with us.

Rejection also teaches us that no one is responsible for another's feelings. Instilled within us is the false notion that we are responsible for other people's feelings. Absurd! We are not responsible for the way they feel about us, and they are not responsible for the way we feel about them. Once we understand that truism, we are free of any unnecessary worry or fear about what others think of us. They are then at liberty to accept us or reject us, and we are freed from the responsibility of trying to alter our lives to fit their expectations.

Now, in order to cope with the rejection we all experience, we must find people who will always accept us and places where we are never rejected. There are some people who will love you unconditionally. There aren't many, but there are some. You may not deserve it, but they will love you anyway.

These people make up a very significant and essential support system.

And there are places where you are never rejected—churches that say, "We don't care what you've done or where you've been or what problems you may have in your life. You are accepted here."

Not long ago someone said to me, "There is no other place in the world where I feel so totally and completely accepted as I do in my church. In spite of all my many problems, I'm never rejected. I'm always accepted and loved." That's what a church is supposed to do.

There is a sign on the lawn of a church in New Jersey: "We reserve the right to accept everybody." That sign ought to appear in front of every church. Find a church that never rejects you.

Also, find a God who never rejects you. Some people don't have a God like that. Their God is so fraught with judgment and punishment that their most painful rejections are those they feel from God. Find a God who accepts you and never rejects you, for God's acceptance allows us to nurture our value, our worth, our self-esteem. It gives us the internal security that allows us to be rejected without being devastated.

Paul Tillich once said that when we experience the ultimate acceptance—God's acceptance—we can love others without being sure of their answering love.

One of my favorite people in show business is Lena Horne. A few years ago she granted an interview to *New York* magazine. In response to a reporter's question, Miss Horne related a conversation with her mother:

It happened just a few years before she died. . . . I said, "Mommy, do you love me?" and she said, "No." I just broke down. "Lena, I wanted a career," she told me. . . . I asked her, "Why did you have me?" and she said, ". . . We wanted a boy and we got you and you got my career." . . .

"Mommy," I told her, "I didn't want the career. . . . I only wanted you to love me. . . ." My mother looked at me and said, "It's over now, Lena. Just forget about it." (May 4, 1981, p. 20)

What tragic, devastating rejection! If I had the privilege of speaking to Lena Horne and to each of you, I would say, "Although your mother may not love you, God does. God loves you; God accepts you; God will never reject you. God will never turn you away—never. Not you, Lena Horne, nor you, nor you, nor you."

PHILIPPIANS 4:11-13

Discontent. In Philippians 4:11*b,* Paul writes, "I have learned, in whatever state I am, to be content" (RŚV). That's an amazing declaration, isn't it? Because we live in an age of discontent, those words strike a responsive chord in our minds and hearts.

Today some of us are dissatisfied all the time, and all of us are dissatisfied some of the time. There is no one who escapes the problem of discontent. Sometimes we find no gratification in our jobs, our families, our friends, our social position, or our financial status. Often we are displeased with our interior selves; we are impatient or angry or guilty or frustrated or unhappy or empty, and we feel discontented with the person we are.

We are often restive in other ways. Some are discontented because they are too young—too young to get a driver's license, too young to date. Many are discontented because they are too short or too tall or too fat or too thin. We just can't seem to put it all together and find the continuing contentment we desire.

In *Gift from the Sea* (Pantheon, 1955), Anne Morrow Lindbergh wrote about the alternating cycles of life—the times when everything is just right and we're so contented we seem "borne along as on a great tide." Then the cycle changes and everything goes wrong. We are so frustrated, unhappy, and discontented "we can't even tie our shoelaces" (p. 24). Those are perceptive observations because that's very much the way it is with most of us. We experience both contentment and discontent simply because we are human. It is a part of our human predicament.

Yet discontent is a destructive force in our lives. It shatters our healthy self-esteem. It destroys our gratitude for life, obliterates our joy and happiness. It harms our relationships with others, even those we cherish most. It diminishes our capacity to be our best selves. And strangely enough, discontent destroys our ability to find contentment.

Granted, contentment is sometimes hard to find. Shakespeare wrote, "My crown is called content: A crown it is that seldom kings enjoy" (*King Henry VI*, Part 3, act 3, sc. 1, lines 64-65). Commoners are also hard-pressed to find it. We seek, we search, we look everywhere to discover the contentment we do not have.

Let me say that, contrary to what many people think, being a Christian will not guarantee contentment. Some preachers preach that it will; some Bible teachers teach that it will; but it will not. I know people who have tried Christianity very much as they would try hot tea, because someone had told them they would be contented all the time. Not so! However, Christianity does enable us to find a solution to our dissatisfaction, because the Christian faith has an answer for discontent.

The apostle Paul sought to win friends, but he made enemies. In his travels to spread the gospel, he was shipwrecked, persecuted, imprisoned. He wanted only to serve Christ, but he was executed. Yet through it all, he could say, "I have learned, in whatever state I am, to be content."

How was that possible? Perhaps the key is in the phrase "I have learned . . . ." If Paul could *learn* the secret of contentment, perhaps we can learn it from him.

In looking at Paul's life, we find he learned to make peace with reality. This must be an elusive lesson because many people live in a dream world, a world that is merely a figment of their imagination, a world that enables them to escape the harsh facts of reality. We are victimized by the distorted picture of life vividly painted by the movies, television, magazines, novels. When we "wish upon a star," our dreams will come true, according to an old song. I wish these words were more than romanticized lyrics, but they are not. The fact is, we cannot wish our dreams true. And we are victimized not only by a dream world, but by our own idealism. We try to live a utopianized life which fails to accommodate itself to the fact that we are imperfect human beings in a less-than-perfect world.

Every counselor knows the problems of persons who are separated from reality. These people are often in a business or job where they must work in concert with others. They fail in their professions for the simple reason that they expect the world to get along with them, when in fact, we all must learn to get along with the world. There is no way to escape the real world. Life is often a diary in which we intend to write one story but are forced to write another. And our story must be one of reality.

Some years ago I preached for several nights in a church where a friend of mine was the minister. In the afternoons we would visit members of his congregation. One day he drove me along a country road to a narrow lane. When we had gone down the lane about as far as we could go, he stopped, led me across a barbed-wire fence and up a narrow pathway to a one-room shack.

The occupant had seen us coming and was waiting at the door. My friend introduced me to the man, probably in his sixties. He was wearing overalls and smoking a pipe. We walked in and were seated in two of the three chairs. I was astounded when I glanced at the wall of that shanty and saw bookshelves containing one of the finest libraries I have ever seen. All the literary classics were there. My eyes kept returning to that wall of books, going from title to title.

When we left, the minister explained: "That man has a Doctor of Philosophy in history from Harvard. He was a professor at one of the great universities, but he could not cope with the realities of the world. He quit and became a recluse. He lives alone and never has any interaction with the real world."

Some people try to escape from reality. Anthony Euwer had a much more healthy outlook:

> As a beauty I am not a great star,
> There are others more handsome by far;
> But my face—I don't mind it,
> For I am behind it.
> It's the people in front that I jar.

I once heard a person say, "What a wonderful life I've had. I only wish I had realized it sooner!" We are often so concerned with a dream world, victimized by a world that does not exist in our futile attempts to escape from the real world, we are unaware that we have a very good life after all.

Paul learned the realities of life the hard way. He wanted everyone to hear the good news gladly, to accept him in love as the servant of God, to trust Jesus Christ as Lord and Savior. But that's not the way it was. And that's not the way it is. Contentment demands the recognition of reality. Paul learned that, and so can we.

Paul also learned the necessity for courage. He said, "I know now how to live when things are difficult and . . . when things are prosperous. . . . I have learned the secret of . . . facing either poverty or plenty" (Phil. 4:12 Phillips).

I am constantly amazed at our capacity for courage. The human body, the human spirit, the human mind have astounding stores of courage in the face of incredible burdens, pressures, and suffering. God has given us the faculty for valor.

Doubtless, Helen Keller will be the greatest woman of her century. Unable to see or hear or speak, she answered that although she did not know the meaning of the darkness, she had learned to overcome it; through her handicaps she had found herself and her God. What great courage! She could have said it another way—"I have learned, in whatever state I am, to be content."

Some time ago I shared my life, as best I could, with a wonderful woman who was dying of cancer. She went through the process of dying for three years. She would go to the hospital for weeks at a time, be released, then be hospitalized again for a different treatment. Each time she lost a bit of vigor and health, but she never lost her spirit, her optimism, her cheerfulness, her radiance. I often asked myself, "How can she take any more? How can she manage another round of treatments? When is she going to give up?" But she never did!

I visited her just a few days before her death. I knew it might be the last time I would see her. And she, too, was aware of this. It was obvious the end was near. Yet she never mentioned that finality. She was smiling, optimistic, radiant. She told me about a new treatment she had just heard of. When I left, I thought of Paul's words. She might have said, "I have learned, in whatever state I am, to be content."

Paul learned the necessity of courage in order to be content; others have learned it, and so can we.

Paul also learned the need for constancy. When people did not respond to him as he wished, it would have been so easy to give up. After all, a preacher is not responsible for the response of the congregation— only for delivering the message.

Paul could have said, "Lord, I've preached the good news of the gospel. These people don't want to hear it; they're not going to respond to it, so I quit. I'm through!" But he didn't do that. Amid disappointment and frustration, surrounded by enemies, he never wavered, never doubted, never capitulated. From constancy, he learned contentment.

I've always had great admiration for prisoners of war—those in World War II, Vietnam, or any other conflict. Day by day, hour by hour, they are under constant temptation to recant, to say what their captors want them to say, in the hope that they may curry favor and receive more lenient treatment. My admiration knows no limits for those who maintained their convictions, their loyalty. When they were released, I think they must have felt a deep sense of inner contentment. Constancy always results in contentment.

Author A. J. Cronin, who was born in a small mining town in South Wales, tells about a cave-in that trapped fourteen miners. Rescuers worked around the clock—24 hours, 48 hours, 72 hours—but still had not reached the trapped men. On the fourth day they wondered if the miners were still alive. They listened for any sound. Finally, as they dug closer, they could hear the men singing:

> O God, our help in ages past,
> Our hope for years to come,
> Our shelter from the stormy blast,
> And our eternal home!

When at last the miners were rescued, they said they had decided to stay constant in their faith. Once they had made that decision, they felt an inner peace, a contentment, and incredibly enough, they said it did not make any difference whether they lived or died.

Paul learned the power of commitment. His commitment contributed to his ability to say, "I have learned, in whatever state I am, to be content." People who are chronically discontented are almost always those who have no overriding commitment to anything beyond themselves, no total surrender to any cause. Sara Henderson Hay described this lack of commitment in "Heresy Indeed":

> It is a piteous thing to be
> Enlisted in no cause at all,
> Unsworn to any heraldry,
> To fly no banner from the wall,
> Own nothing you would sweat or try for,
> Or bruise your hands, or bleed, or die for.
>
> . . . .
>
> Ah, this were heresy indeed,
> That all God's pity will not stay for,
> And your immortal soul will pay for.

If you are discontented, ask yourself this. Is there "nothing you would sweat or try for, or bruise your hands, or bleed, or die for"? Paul was totally committed to the good news of Jesus Christ: "I can do all things in him who strengthens me" (Phil. 4:13 RSV). Paul was totally contented because he was totally committed.

Some years ago I knew of a man who lived in an elegant home and enjoyed every comfort. He possessed everything we would think of as desirable. But he was discontented. He realized he needed a new and total commitment to a cause beyond himself. So he went to India as a missionary. He labored there for many years, finding total contentment in the power of a total commitment.

I'm not suggesting that anyone give up a job and go to India as a missionary. However, if you are not totally committed to some great cause beyond yourself, you are missing total contentment. Contentment is not a human achievement. It is a divine gift. It is not the result of being self-sufficient. It is the result of being God-sufficient. It comes from being able to live, as well as to sing,

> Lord, I would place my hand in thine,
> Nor ever murmur nor repine;
> Content, whatever lot I see,
> Since 'tis my God that leadeth me.

Paul learned, and so can we. It is truly a great day when a person can honestly say, "I have learned, in whatever state I am, to be content."

I JOHN 1:9
ROMANS 5:21

Guilt.   When was the last time you felt guilty? Was
it last week, yesterday, or ten minutes ago? Because we
are human, all of us suffer pangs of guilt at one time or
another. We feel guilty because of our sins, whether
they are real or imagined. Most of us are aware that
there are real sins—sins of omission, sins of commis-
sion, and sometimes sins of submission.

However, there are also imagined sins. At times
we feel guilty for things that are not really wrong at all.
Or we feel guilty for sins that have already been
forgiven. We suffer self-imposed guilt.

This aspect of our human predicament is more
than unfortunate, because there is probably nothing
more totally destructive to the human psyche, the
human mind, or even the human body, than guilt.
Guilt does things to us that God never intended. It is
self-destructive, it enslaves us, it burdens us. It
destroys our freedom, and it spawns fear, worry, and
inferiority.

Our guilt is also "other" destructive. In extreme
cases, we can drag our guilt around and let it pile up

until we feel we have to project it onto someone else to get rid of it. By doing so, we hope to relieve ourselves of the burden. So in a very real sense, guilt is both suicidal and homicidal. It can destroy us and it can destroy others.

In order to avoid the destructiveness of guilt, we need to understand something about its psychology. Guilt is often self-validating. When we feel guilty, we tell ourselves, "I really am bad. I actually do have a tainted character. I'm an evil person." It is also self-punishing. Often people feel, "I've paid the price. I'm suffering for my guilt."

And guilt can be self-rewarding. At times, we want to be guilty. We are unhappy unless we are guilty. We somehow think we ought to feel guilty, and when we don't, we feel guilty because we're not guilty. This cycle can perpetuate itself and devastate us.

Many authors and playwrights have dealt with the subject. And throughout the centuries, philosophers, theologians, psychologists, and psychiatrists have recognized the destructiveness of guilt. And due in large part to this awareness, numerous solutions have been proposed to assuage, diminish, and combat our guilt.

For instance, a New Jersey artist recently developed a disposable guilt bag, available through a mail-order catalogue. The instructions read, "Place bag securely over mouth. Blow guilt away. Dispose of bag immediately." Twenty-five-hundred kits of ten bags each have been sold as of this writing, and according to an Associated Press report, several famous people have purchased the kits.

Obviously, people are searching for ways to dispose of their guilt. It is true that we must get rid of it, for guilt is unhealthy and unnecessary. It is of absolutely no use, except as it sensitizes our consciences to our moral and ethical responsibilities.

What is the answer? There is only one! And it is contained in these verses of Scripture: "If we confess our sins, he is faithful and just, and will forgive our sins" (I John 1:9 RSV); "Where sin abounded, grace did much more abound" (Rom. 5:20*b*). Verse after verse of holy Scripture speaks to us of God's forgiveness and grace. In the New Testament, the word *guilt* is found eight times; the word *forgiveness,* seventy-one.

To be sure, some people would have us believe that God is primarily interested in convicting us of our sins and making us feel guilty. But the New Testament affirms that God is more interested in forgiving sins and erasing guilt. God promises forgiveness of sins, release from guilt, and life under grace.

One of the most incredible statements in the Bible is found in the book of Jeremiah. God says, "I will forgive their iniquity, and I will remember their sin no more" (31:34*c*). Think of that! We can't do that, but God can. It is a part of his divine nature that he not only forgives sins but forgets them, totally and completely. "As the heavens are high above the earth . . . as far as the east is from the west, so far does he remove our transgressions from us" (Ps. 103:11, 12 RSV). Only God can do that. We can be set free from our guilt only through God's forgiveness.

Furthermore, that forgiveness manifests itself in several ways. First of all, it frees us from the doubts that destroy faith. Guilt creates doubt, and doubt destroys faith. This is the way it might work: Some people may not feel good about God, because they do not feel good about themselves; guilt has created the doubts that destroy faith. Others may not believe in God's forgiveness because they do not find it possible to forgive themselves; again, guilt has created the doubts that destroy faith. Still others may doubt God's goodness because they doubt their own goodness; if this is the case, again guilt has created the doubts that destroy faith.

Some years ago a man told me he could not become a Christian. He could not accept Christ because he could never believe that God could actually forgive his sins—they were too terrible, beyond forgiveness. His guilt had created doubts that destroyed his faith.

After Peter betrayed Jesus, the doubts created by guilt would have destroyed his faith, had he not experienced total forgiveness. The woman at the well could not have become a follower of Christ unless she had known the forgiveness that freed her from the guilt that created doubts about her faith.

Forgiveness also frees us from the sins that feed on our guilt. Guilt increases fear, intensifies worry, magnifies our sense of inferiority, and deepens our depression.

My wife and I are the parents of twin boys. One night after they received their driver's licenses, they wanted to take the car out by themselves. They had no experience driving after dark, but in a moment of weakness I let them go, with the understanding that they would be home promptly by 10:00 P.M. They were not home at 10:00. Nor were they home by 10:15 or 10:30.

Then my guilt set in. I was already worried and fearful, but then I began to feel guilty. I thought, "I knew better than that. I shouldn't have done it. It's my fault." My guilt fed my fears and worries. When the boys finally came home, I was distraught. My nervousness and distress had been intensified by my sense of guilt.

But forgiveness frees us from the problems that feed on our guilt. If we have low self-esteem, a sense of guilt will make it worse. If we have reason to be depressed, a sense of guilt will make us more depressed. However, forgiveness can liberate us from these attendant problems.

Forgiveness also frees us to establish good relationships with others. The destructiveness of guilt is not limited to ourselves; it extends to others. When we are paralyzed by the effects of guilt, we become unattractive to others. We may not know why, and they may not know why, but we appear less than appealing.

Moreover, in its extreme form, as mentioned previously, guilt may make us want everyone else to feel guilty. In fact, many people who are hypercritical, always criticizing, condemning, accusing, judging, do so because they are burdened with an unbearable load of guilt. Their guilt has become so heavy they try to project it, dump it onto others. They do this to rid themselves of the guilt, but their attempts are in vain, and so they feel more guilty.

When Flip Wilson said, "The devil made me do it!" he was revealing a tremendously important theological insight. He was, in effect, dumping his guilt on the devil. Once in a while I hear someone say "Satan made me do it" or "The anti-Christ made me do it."

Perhaps not in such obvious ways, but more often than we realize, we all try to project our guilt onto something or someone else. We say "My mother is at fault," "My brother," "My boss"—we project our guilt onto them. When the thief on the cross said, "If thou be the Christ, save thyself and us," he was trying to get rid of his own guilt. And when Pilate could find nothing wrong with the Christ, yet sentenced him to die, he was saying, "I'm not guilty. They made me do it. They forced me into it."

The destructiveness of guilt in our relationships with others is serious indeed. We desperately need the forgiveness that frees us for a healthy relationship with other people.

Finally, forgiveness frees us for new life in Jesus Christ. Jesus said, "I am come that they might have life, and that they might have it more abundantly" (John 10:10b). But we do not enter into that abundant life until we first have walked through the gates of confession and repentance, and have accepted God's forgiveness. Although that forgiveness is free, we often don't accept it. However, "If we confess our sins, he is faithful and just to forgive us our sins, and to cleanse us from all unrighteousness" (I John 1:9). "Where sin abounds, grace does much more abound" (Rom. 5:21). After accepting God's forgiveness, we are free to receive and possess life abundant, be the persons we can be, the persons God intended us to be.

The choice is ours. We don't need to stay locked in the prison of guilt. We don't need to continue to carry the staggering burden of guilt. We don't need to be paralyzed by its destructive effects. We can be free to laugh and play and enter the abundance of life that Christ promised. But forgiveness, only forgiveness, frees us for that.

When Alonzo Mann was a boy, he witnessed the murder of a young girl. He knew the murderer might take his life if he reported what he had seen. Subsequently, a man named Leo Frank, a Jew, was arrested for the murder of the little girl. He was tried, convicted, and sentenced to death. A band of vigilantes broke into the jail and killed Leo Frank. Seventy years later, Alonzo Mann stood at the grave of the murdered girl.

He said, "It was not Leo Frank. For seventy years I have lived with my guilt. At last I am free of it." (Some time later, Leo Frank was pardoned posthumously.)

What a tragedy! Seventy years of previous life wasted by guilt! But we don't need to wait 70 years or 70 minutes, or even 70 seconds. Right now, in the twinkling of an eye or the turning of a thought, each of us can accept the forgiveness God offers and begin a new life in Christ, free forever of the terrifying force of guilt.

> Amazing grace! How sweet the sound
> That saved a wretch like me!
> I once was lost, but now am found,
> Was blind, but now I see.

JOHN 20:24-29
JOHN 11:16

Doubt. If asked to name the twelve disciples, most of us probably would hastily decline. Yet we are very familiar with one of them. We frequently invoke his name when we refer to someone who questions; his name is part of our vocabulary—Doubting Thomas, our synonym for a skeptic.

Due to that appellation, many do not think too highly of Thomas. This assessment is unfair because, in fact, Thomas was a rather remarkable disciple. He was courageous, loyal, candid, and open.

When Jesus resolved to return to Judea from beyond the Jordan, it was Thomas who said to the other disciples, "Let us all go and die with him" (John 11:16 Phillips). And when Jesus was trying to point the way to the Father's house, Thomas was candid enough to say, "Lord, we do not know where you are going; how can we know the way?" (John 14:5 RSV). When they told him Jesus was alive, Thomas said he would not believe until he saw for himself. But when Thomas was able to feel the nail prints in Christ's hands and the spear mark in his side, he made this magnificent confession of faith—"My Lord and my God" (John 20:28b). Nonetheless, he is known primarily as Doubting Thomas, and it is in that role that he is instructive for us.

To be sure, there are some who never have doubts. I have heard people say, "I've never had a doubt in my life. I find it easy to believe, and I am never afflicted with any doubts." To them, I would say Congratulations! If you are one of those people, skip this chapter. However, because we are only human, most of us do have some doubts. Personally, I find I am more akin to Doubting Thomas than to the other disciples, for I have doubted my way into faith. I find it very difficult to accept without first doubting.

Not long ago a woman said to me, "I have never had a doubt about the Christian faith in all my life until now. Can you believe it? I'm ninety-two, and I'm just beginning to doubt the existence of God."

My answer was, "Be grateful. Most of us have been doing that for years." Paul Tournier said that those who claim never to doubt do not know what faith is, for faith is forged through doubt (*The Person Reborn*, 1975).

Now, we do need to be aware of several things while we are struggling with our doubt. First of all, we need to remember that doubt is a compliment to our intellect. It is said that Clarence Darrow, the famous atheist, once remarked during a debate, "They tell me there is a God, but I've never seen him." To which Roy L. Smith replied, "It is credibly reported that Mr. Clarence Darrow has a mind, but I've never seen it."

The point is that Thomas was willing to question, and doubt is a compliment to our intellect because that means we are willing to ask questions. Thomas questioned—"I'm not going to believe just because you say so. Let me see him; let me feel him; let me touch him."

In retrospect, I believe the best students in school are the ones who ask questions. Remarkable advances have been made by the human race because doubt has motivated persons to question. In science, technology, medicine, theology, much of the progress has been made by those willing to ask questions.

At one time most people sincerely believed the world was flat. But a few doubted—"Is the world really flat?" Others asked, "Is the earth the center of the universe?" "Is God an invention of the human mind?" "Is the universe as uncaring as some say?" "Is there really no meaning to human existence?" "Is it really true that no human being can go to the moon or launch satellites or build laboratories and live in space?" "Is it really true that there is no cure for cancer?" Because that question has been asked, millions of dollars are being spent to search for cures for cancer and other diseases. Enormous progress is being made because persons with intelligence have doubted and been willing to question. "Is it necessary that some people in the world go hungry?" "Must human beings settle their differences by war?" "Is this earthly life really all there is?"

You see, doubt is a compliment to your intellect because it motivates you to challenge assumptions heretofore thought to be valid.

Another advantage of doubt is that it is an antidote for apathy. It is so easy to become unconcerned. Thomas, who was absent at the first post-resurrection appearance of Jesus, withdrew. He became apathetic. It is quite easy for us to surrender to what we term the inevitables of life—the poor are always with us; there will always be war and rumors of war. I even heard a clergyman say, "There's no point in worrying about war; the Bible says we'll always have it."

In a more personal vein, we say, "I've always been like this. It's one of my family traits, so there's no use trying to do anything about it." There is always the temptation to be apathetic. I've heard people say, "I believe this is the way life is. I've never thought to question it." We are neutral about our religious beliefs, so we never challenge them. That's where honest doubt is good. Honest doubt is an antidote to our apathy. It motivates us to ask questions.

I once heard a man relate an interesting story: "I thought I had to live in the gutter. For years I accepted that with total apathy, because I had been trained to believe that my fate was the result of both heredity and environment. And then one day I began to doubt that. I began to wonder if a person could overcome both those strong forces. And I discovered I could be different. I overcame my apathy through my doubts."

Doubt is also a test for doubt. If we test our faith by our doubts, why isn't it reasonable to test our doubts by our doubts?

Thomas was a complete realist. He reasoned, and rightly so, that any man who talked, taught, and lived as Jesus did was headed for the cross. That made good sense. So when he heard that Jesus had appeared again after his death, this really disturbed Thomas. He began to think, "Maybe I was wrong. Perhaps it is possible for him to be alive again. Understand—I want proof. But maybe I should doubt my doubts."

This questioning of our doubts occurs frequently in many areas of our lives. Some of us, at least at some point in our lives, doubt that school is of any value. Maybe you didn't go through that, but I did. There was a period when I doubted that school could add anything to the marvelous intelligence I already possessed. I especially doubted my parents' insistence that I take four years of Latin. I thought it was a dead language; nobody even spoke it; it was a total waste of time. I had very, very strong doubts about the wisdom of taking any Latin at all. But after about two years, I began to reap some of the rewards of being exposed to that language. I was learning the etymology of words, particularly the interesting English derivatives. I began to doubt my doubts, and from doubting my doubts, I came to have absolute faith in the value of studying Latin.

Little boys, at one time in their lives, have doubts about little girls. When our boys were small, they wouldn't invite girls to their parties. But when they were about fourteen, they began to doubt their doubts. Suddenly we had a different problem—they didn't want to invite any boys.

Several years ago a man who had experienced shattering disappointment said to me, "If God would allow this to happen in my life, there is no God." I was able to convince that man to doubt his doubts. Finally he was able to see that it takes a lot more blind faith to disbelieve in God than it does to believe in God. Doubt is a test of faith. Why not use it as a test of our doubts?

In *How Great Christians Met Christ,* James C. Hefley describes Charles Finney as a highly intelligent young lawyer, and a fine musician as well. He had the charismatic personality of a leader. He became a skeptic, a cynic, an agnostic. He had fun with the crowd of young people in the village where he lived and worked. They all liked him, and they prayed he would regain his faith. More than anything else, he enjoyed reading Blackstone's law books. In those books he discovered not only constant references to the Bible, but a reverence and an acceptance of its authority. Thus Charles Finney began to read the Bible, and he began to doubt his doubts.

He decided it wasn't the Bible's fault that so many Christians didn't live like Christians, and he plugged up the keyhole in his law office door so no one would hear him praying. He became convinced that here, indeed and in truth, was the way of life. Shortly thereafter, he dedicated himself to the God who reveals himself in the person of Jesus Christ. Soon almost the entire town was converted under Charles Finney's dynamic preaching. All of New England was impressed with the power of his witness. Even today the sermons and lectures of Charles Finney are preserved and read. And he came to his faith through doubting his doubts ([Moody Press, 1973], pp. 75-77).

Finally, doubt is a reason to try faith. On John Wesley's voyage to Georgia, the small ship on which he had sailed encountered a great storm. It appeared all aboard would be drowned. Wesley was fearful and worried, but he noticed some Moravian passengers who were very calm, poised, and self-assured.

Later in England, Wesley met Peter Böhler, a Moravian clergyman, who explained that calmness: "When your doubts are greatest, that's the time to try faith. Preach faith," he said, "and you'll find you have faith."

That is reminiscent of Jesus' statement, paraphrased by Dietrich Bonhoeffer in *The Cost of Discipleship:* "Do not say you have not got faith. You will not have it so long as you persist in disobedience and refuse to take the first step." In other words, "When you doubt, try faith."

Everybody doubted that an airplane could fly. Even the Wright brothers had doubts, but, partially because everyone said it couldn't be done, they decided to try. And they succeeded. I recently read about the man who invented big-screen television. Almost everyone said, "There's no way," but he tried, and he succeeded.

This same reckoning is true in our personal life and in our religious life. When we have the worst doubts—that's the time to try faith. When we are devastated, destroyed by sorrow, some vast disappointment, or inexplicable tragedy; when we feel like crying out, "Where are you, God? Why did you let this happen to me? I really don't believe in God any more!"; when doubt is at its highest level—that's the time to try faith. That time probably will come to all of us. There will be some critical moment when the world falls apart and there is no apparent reason to continue to believe in God's goodness or love. When we are filled with doubt—that's when we need to try faith.

Borrow some faith, if necessary. Thank goodness I've been able to borrow money a few times. It has saved my life. My life also has been saved when I've been able to borrow someone's faith. My rationale at such times: If they say it's true, then I'll accept it; I will usc their belief for a while until I get my own back. That's what it means to say that doubt is a reason to try faith.

"The life I now live in the flesh," Paul said, "I live by faith in the Son of God" (Gal. 2:20c RSV). Sometimes we must live by the faith of a God we do not really believe in at that moment, until we find our way back to our own faith.

James Hefley also tells the story of Adoniram Judson, son of a clergyman. He had a brilliant mind, went to Brown University, and graduated with honors. Early in his college career, he came to know Jacob Eames, and they became the greatest of friends. Jacob Eames was an agnostic. Through his influence, Adoniram Judson too became an agnostic. He tried to keep this from his father and mother, but his decision to go to New York City and write for the stage was the final blow to his parents.

In the ensuing argument he blurted out that their God was not his God, that he did not believe in the Bible or in the divinity of Jesus Christ.

Subsequently, unable to fulfill his dreams of success in New York, Judson, in frustration, wandered throughout the country. One evening he stayed at a village inn. The desk clerk assigned him to the only available room—next to one in which a man was dying. The clerk apologized, but Judson did not care; he was tired and wanted to rest. Yet sleep eluded him. From the next room came the moans and groans of the dying man, mingled with the hustle and bustle of people going in and out.

The next morning he asked the desk clerk, "How is the sick man?"

"Dead," the clerk replied somberly.

"Too bad," Adoniram responded. "Did you know him?"

"He registered as Jacob Eames," the clerk answered.

Judson began to consider his doubts. Was Jacob Eames really right? Was there no God, no Christ, no life beyond the grave? And in that moment, Judson decided to try faith once again, to experiment with experience. How does it feel to really believe in a God who is goodness, love, and power? How does it feel to believe in a Christ who rose from the dead? In experimenting with experience, he discovered the truth of his faith. He became a clergyman and was offered the largest pulpit in Boston, but he turned it down.

Twelve days after their marriage, he and his wife sailed for Burma, where he served as a missionary. There he was tortured and imprisoned and, to add discouragement to injury, it was six years before he won his first convert. Nonetheless, Judson never again gave up his belief—in all probability, because when his doubt was at its worst, he tried faith. By experimenting with experience, he discovered it was true (pp. 59-62).

Doubts? To be sure! I never expect to be rid of them all. They will continue to come back again and again. Still, we can affirm these lines with Mary Gardiner Brainard:

> So I go on not knowing—I would not if I might;
> I would rather walk in the dark with God
>   than go alone in the light;
> I would rather walk with Him by faith
>   than walk alone by sight.
>
> —"Not Knowing"

PSALM 42:5
ROMANS 8:24

Despair.
In Psalm 42, the psalmist declared, "Hope thou in God: for I shall yet praise him, who is the health of my countenance" (vs. 11*b*). In Romans, chapter eight, one of the greatest in the New Testament, the apostle Paul declares, "We are saved by hope" (vs. 24).

The Bible has a great deal to say about hope; its writers understood that we are often subject to despair. Because we are human, we often feel a sense of deep and abiding despondency. Throughout the centuries, men and women have known the experience of despair, and our day is certainly no different.

Even children frequently feel despair. We don't realize this because our children often don't share their feelings with us. However, child psychologists tell us children may feel extreme despair, perhaps because they cannot please their parents or because they cannot compete successfully with their peers or because of the myriad problems they confront as they approach adulthood. Surely all of us are aware of the dramatic increase in the number of suicides among teenagers in the past few years. Some feel despair about preparing for a future they think will never come. Some feel despair about the competition for grades and place. Some feel despair about their appearance. Most feel despair about the pressure of conforming to the value judgments of the crowd.

Men and women in every station of life feel despair. Sometimes they are burned out in their jobs; they no longer find joy in their work or motivation for it. Or perhaps they realize that their dreams for themselves professionally will never come true. There is despair when a home, a family, a marriage breaks up. Sometimes both husband and wife have honestly tried, but to no avail. Then there is despair, a sense of hopelessness.

When we face the death of one whom we love more than life itself—sometimes a child or youth, or a man or woman in the prime of life, we feel desperate despair.

People often feel hopeless when they face retirement, with seemingly nothing to do, no place to go, and an inadequate income for their last years. There is despair when someone is told he or she has a terminal illness; there is loneliness, fear, and, at times, utter despair.

Despair may envelop us gradually, inch by inch, in slow degrees. We see it coming, but we are helpless to prevent it. Or it may surround us with such terrifying suddenness, there is no time to prepare. A doctor may walk into a waiting room and say, "I'm sorry." Despair is our lot because we are human. And along with the despair come devastation and destruction—not only in the number of suicides but in the slow death that often results from despair.

In *Live at Peace with Your Nerves,* Dr. Walter Alvarez wrote about his father, a missionary-physician in the South Seas. There, witch doctors could convince the natives they were going to die, that there was no hope, no help; and they would indeed perish. Persons died for no reason, other than having been told they would. Robbed of their hope, their will to live, they died of despair. I myself once heard of a woman who died, her doctor said, for no reason other than despair. Hopelessness is a cunning assassin.

What is the antidote for our despair? The answer is Christian hope. Christian hope is not, as some believe, a disinclination to take life seriously. It is not living in a Pollyanna world that shuts its eyes to everything ugly. It is not viewing life through rose-colored glasses. Christian hope is not cheerful optimism, but confidence in an ultimate divine destiny—invisible, unseen, unprovable, and unaffected by evil deeds or evil men and women. It is true belief in a God who is sovereign, in control of the universe, invincible, unconquerable. It is the assurance that God and God alone will have the final say about the universe. It is confidence in an ultimate divine destiny, which cannot be frustrated or aborted.

The psalmist says, "Hope thou in God"; Paul says, "We are saved by hope." Yet the question remains—how does hope actually overcome despair?

Hope reminds us to keep life in its proper perspective. It is so easy to get life out of balance, to forget it is a mixture—a potpourri of good and evil, misery and joy, life and death.

When I was a child I thought every good thing that happened to me would be followed by something bad. I remember hoping the bad would hurry up and happen so I could get to the next thing, which would be good. In retrospect, I believe perhaps I was searching for a valid life principle—that life is neither all good nor all bad, but a mixture. Like the spiritual—

> Sometimes I'm up, sometimes I'm down,
> Oh, yes, Lord!
> Sometimes I'm almost to the groun',
> Oh, yes, Lord!

—sometimes life is up, sometimes it's down; it's a mixture. Illness is real, but so is health. Disaster comes, but so does happiness. Death is a fact, but so is life. Yet our tendency seems to be to overrate the bad and underrate the good, to emphasize despair and ignore hope.

An uncle of mine did that. His perspective on life was truly out of balance. Each time he had good fortune, he would discover something bad about it. I have come to wonder whether perhaps he did not die partly from despair because he had such a distorted outlook. He had no confidence in Christian hope, that ultimate divine destiny which has the final say about human life.

I read about a man, the sole survivor of a shipwreck, who was washed up on an uninhabited island. He built a crude hut with the few possessions he was able to salvage. Every day he prayed, and then searched the horizon for a ship that might save him.

But none came. One day, having gone in search of food, he returned to find his hut in flames. Everything was destroyed. He was plunged into abject despair. There was nothing left, only a slow death.

But the next day a ship arrived. The captain said, "We saw your smoke signal!"

It's easy to get a distorted picture of life. "Hope thou in God." We are saved by hope because hope reminds us to keep life in proper perspective.

Hope also reminds us to keep time in proper perspective. Our way of keeping time—in terms of seconds, minutes, hours, and days—is faulty. The Bible is very clear about this: One day is equal to a thousand years. This day, this twenty-four hours, is of relative insignificance. This day is important, but not as important as we tend to make it. This day—this situation, this experience, this tragedy, this crisis—is of relative unimportance, because against the backdrop of eternity, this day is nothing.

At a time when I felt despair and utter hopelessness, I kept saying to myself, "This day is nothing. It is unimportant. This day is insignificant."

Recently, I was talking to a person who felt totally hopeless. I said, "Wait until tomorrow."

He said, "No, there's no tomorrow. This is the end. There is no hope."

The next day when I called him, he said, "You were right. I do feel better today."

Christian hope enables us to keep time in its proper perspective. One event, one situation, one crisis, one defeat, is insignificant when seen on the true stage of time.

A mighty king once decreed that one of his subjects should die.

The poor man begged the king to postpone his execution. "I will teach your horse to fly if you will postpone my death for one year."

A friend asked him, "Why do that? It's inevitable that you are going to die."

"No, it is not inevitable that I should die," the peasant replied. "In fact, the odds are four to one in my favor."

"How do you figure that?" his friend asked.

The peasant answered, "One, the king might die. Two, I might die. Three, the horse might die. And four, I might teach the horse to fly. It's four to one in my favor."

We must try to keep time in its proper framework, and Christian hope allows us to do just that. The disciples were victimized by the misunderstanding of time, much as we are today. At the crucifixion they thought, "This is the end. Our hope is dead." It was not until Easter Sunday that they realized their mistake. "Hope thou in God." We are saved by hope because hope reminds us to keep time in proper perspective.

And hope reminds us to keep our faith in proper perspective. I am always amazed when people talk about having an abundance of faith, but never mention their hope. Surely even a cursory glance at the New Testament will reveal that one cannot have faith without hope. Faith cannot stand on its own. It must have the support of hope.

However, no one can have faith all the time. I don't believe it is possible for people to maintain the maximum potential of faith. If they say they do, you can be assured of one of two things—they are either saints or suspect. It's just not possible for us to always maintain the maximum level of faith. We can't be gung-ho about God all the time. In fact, there are some days when we can hardly believe God even exists. And that's all right, because that's when our faith is sustained and supported by our hope.

The disciples and friends and family of Jesus, watching him die on a cross, thought, "God has betrayed us. Christ is dead. Faith is a fraud." But when their faith was gone, they were sustained by hope—a wild hope, perhaps, but nonetheless hope—that somehow, in some inexplicable way, God might do something, even with the crucified Christ. When we have lost our faith, we must have hope, because hope sustains and supports our faith.

When I stood in the presence of tragedy recently, my mind rebelled at the irrationality and senselessness of what had occurred. My heart screamed, "Why, God? Why?" My faith was weakened, and all I had left was hope. But faith is strengthened, sustained, supported, buoyed by hope. "We are saved by hope." Thomas Merton once wrote that, in the darkness, we are sometimes united to God by hope.

Some of you may have seen the Louvre's dramatic painting of Goethe's *Faust,* in which Mephistopheles, the devil of medieval legend, and Faust are seated at a table with a chessboard between them. The devil is pointing with a leer, and Faust sits dejected. We can almost hear Mephistopheles crying, "Checkmate!"

An internationally known chess player was admiring this magnificent painting when suddenly he lunged forward and exclaimed, "Just a minute! Faust has one more move!"

When faith gives way to despair, just a minute! You have one more move! It is the move of hope. For hope keeps our faith in proper perspective.

Because we are human, there will be times in our lives when we feel despair. If it hasn't come to you yet, you haven't lived long enough. It will come. When it does, remember to "hope thou in God," for "we are saved by hope."

For God created man for incorruption . . . in the image of his own eternity.

—*THE WISDOM OF SOLOMON 2:23 RSV Apocrypha*

For Christ has completely abolished death, and has now, through the gospel, opened to us . . . the shining possibilities of the life that is eternal.

—*II TIMOTHY 1:10 Phillips*

Death is swallowed up in victory. O death, where is thy sting? O grave, where is thy victory?

—*I CORINTHIANS 15:54c-55*

Death. All of us will die some day, simply because

we are human. There is no escape from the mortality of our humanity. The ultimate question of life is the ultimate question of death. All other problems concerned with our human predicament are finally and inextricably tied to this one conclusive question.

Job asked, "If a man die, shall he live again?" (14:14). That is the question millions of people have asked through the ages. Paul Tillich once remarked that the anxiety of death overshadows all other anxieties.

In other words, along with whatever questions we have, there is always this overlay of the question of death. The difficulty we have in facing the possibility and the necessity of our death is indeed a problem for most people. I know very few who are looking forward to it, at least any time soon. I suppose we would agree with Woody Allen: "I don't want immortality through my work. I want immortality through not dying." Most of us would like it that way. No matter what we may say, death is a problem because it is the ultimate question of life.

Have you ever felt that perhaps you were literally at death's door? Or have you ever watched another person die? Do you know the experience of panic, dread, reluctance, and regret that human beings feel when they think they are about to die? Because we all are human, there is no escape—we must face the question of our death.

In the Bible we read, "This mortal must put on immortality" (I Cor. 15:53b); "Christ has completely abolished death, and has now, through the gospel, opened to us men the shining possibilities of the life that is eternal" (II Tim. 1:10 Phillips); "Death is swallowed up in victory" (I Cor. 15:54c). Our faith tells us we shall live on in a personal, conscious life beyond the grave. Yet this is not just a matter of faith, for there is also compelling evidence—evidence in the intellect, the heart, and the conscience—that physical death is not the end, but the beginning of a new and different life.

There is the evidence of the indestructible nature of love. Time and space cannot destroy love. Love in itself possesses an immortality. Death cannot separate us from those we love because death cannot kill what never dies.

The first disciples felt a tremendous bond of love with the risen Christ, and rightly so. It was not only their love for him but, more important, his love for them—a love that could not be destroyed, that was indestructible, imperishable. Paul spoke of this magnificently:

Who shall separate us from the love of Christ? Shall tribulation, or distress, or persecution, or famine, or nakedness, or peril, or sword? . . . Nay, in all these things we are more than conquerors through him that loved us. For I am persuaded, that neither death, nor life, nor angels, nor principalities, nor powers, nor things present, nor things to come, nor height, nor depth, nor any other creature, shall be able to separate us from the love of God, which is in Christ Jesus our Lord. (Rom. 8:35, 37-39)

I always read those words at a funeral service. Each time, I am amazed at their freshness; love is indestructible, and nothing can separate us from the love of God, not even death. And nothing can separate us from the love of those we love, because while that love is but a dim reflection of God's love, it also is indestructible.

The understanding of the indestructibility of love offers compelling evidence of life beyond the grave.

There is also imperative evidence in the nature of human beings. Our intrinsic worth is at the core of biblical teaching. We are created by God. We are made in his image. The breath of his divinity has been breathed into us. The Christian faith believes that human personality has incalculable worth. We believe we are valuable not because of what we produce or contribute, but because we are created of God, made in his image.

That's the difference between Marxism and Christianity. Communism believes that a human being has worth only in regard to what he or she can contribute. Those who no longer contribute can be easily replaced, like cogs in a machine. In Christianity, each person has inherent worth in the sight of God.

Jesus said, "There is a joy in heaven over just one sinner who repents." If humans have this kind of value in the sight of God, then it is inconceivable that death should be the end, that a human being could be blown out of existence as we would extinguish a candle's flame. Not only is it inconceivable, it is also irrational.

Would God do that to us? Having made us, having created us, having fashioned us through years of this earthly existence, at the end does he simply extinguish us like a candle's flame, ashes to ashes? Would a parent do that to a child? Is it not blasphemous to believe he would?

To be sure, if our lives could be finished at the end of our earthly existence, perhaps it would make some sense, but no person's life is ever finished. No matter how long you live, no matter how well you live, at the conclusion of your earthly existence, your life is still an unfinished symphony. As long as it is, a God who created you, who stamped you with his own divinity, will not leave you in dust and ashes.

And there is evidence of life beyond the grave in the character of God. God has a character, and some things are patently inconsonant with that character. To the Sadducees who did not believe in the resurrection of the dead, Jesus declared that God "is not the God of the dead, but the God of the living" (Mark 12:27). It is inconsistent with the character of God to believe that God is the God of the dead. And it would be a denial of his character to imply that his children could ever be overcome by death.

If we were to believe that, think what it implies: that God has used all preceding generations of humankind merely as fertilizer for the universe. That is an abysmally pagan idea, an utter blasphemy of God and the utter degradation of man.

Indeed, God's nature, by very definition, can contain no more love than our nature contains. Certainly the character of God and the character of love would not allow that. A rock is immortal. The chemical properties of a rock cannot be destroyed. Is it conceivable that God would make a rock immortal, but would not give immortality to a little child, who can love and pray and laugh and cry? "If a man die, shall he live again?" The answer to that is found in the character of God.

Furthermore, there is the answer of the resurrected Christ. The first disciples were not unmindful of evidences of immortality. But the irrefutable proof was in the resurrection of Jesus Christ. When they saw that the cross and the tomb could not hold him; when they saw and talked with him, their faith became a certainty. What they had believed by faith, they now knew by experience. Through the pages of the New Testament and through the witness of the early church, they proclaimed the glorious news that death is not the end of life.

On the tombstones in ancient cemeteries, certain letters were often engraved—NF F NS NC. They stood for the Latin *non fui, fui, non sum, non curo* (I was not, I was, I am not, I do not care)—a hopeless, cynical commentary. There was no hope beyond the grave. But that was B.C., Before Christ, and now Christ has risen; Christ is alive, and there is the assurance of immortality. For Christ has completely abolished death through his resurrection, has opened to us the shining possibilities of life that is eternal. "If a man die, shall he live again?" The resurrected Christ answers an emphatic Yes!

In Bach's magnificent *Passion According to St. John*, there is an alto aria on Jesus' words from the cross, "It is finished." As the solo begins, the audience can feel the sobbing throb of humanity—"It is finished, finished." Suddenly the trumpets sound and the soloist sings fortissimo, "The Lion of Judah has conquered" (in the background, the lament of humanity; above it, the notes of the trumpet). "The Lion of Judah has conquered."

"If a man die, shall he live again?" The Easter answer is "Yes, in a personal, conscious life beyond the grave. Hallelujah! Hallelujah! Hallelujah!"